COOL TRICKS!

A Grown-Up's Guide to All the Neat Things You Never Learned to Do as a Kid!

•

JOHN JAVNA

CB

CONTEMPORARY
BOOKS

CHICAGO · NEW YORK

Library of Congress Cataloging-in-Publication Data

Javna, John.
  Cool tricks.
  1. Amusements.   2. Tricks.   3. Games.   I. Title.
GV1201.J35   1989   793   89-15701
ISBN 0-8092-4422-5

To Miss Borowski and Miss Reese, for no particular reason, except that I remember them

Produced and packaged by Javnarama
Design by Javnarama

Published by Contemporary Books, Inc.
Two Prudential Plaza, Chicago, Illinois 60601-6790
Manufactured in the United States of America
International Standard Book Number: 0-8092-4422-5

CONTENTS

INTRODUCTION

About 10 books ago, I discovered an important lesson for authors: The subject you write about is the subject you learn about. If an author writes about atomic energy, he or she inevitably becomes an expert in that field. If an author winds up putting together a book on 65 uses for possum fat—well, that's the subject he or she is stuck with.

So this time, I wrote about having fun. And it worked...sort of. Writing the book was still hard work. But when each section was completed, I'd learned something I could entertain myself and my kids with. I juggle all the time now, for exam-ple—although I'm still not very good at it. And I love making dollar bow ties for just about anyone who'll stand still long enough for me to finish the trick.

I'm not going through a second childhood yet. But I am approaching 40, if that explains anything.

Still, I'm not sure if the inspiration for this book was my 38th birth-day...or a realization that I'd forgotten how to do all the neat things I spent hours and hours mastering as a child. For some reason, as people get older, we seem to feel less comfortable engaging in low-tech activities whose only purpose is to make us giggle. But here's a pleasant surprise from someone who's spent the last 6 months yo-yoing and making giant bubbles: It's still fun. You won't want to spend every waking hour trying to "walk the dog." But even 15 minutes of kid stuff is great for the soul.

Still need a reason to make a balloon animal or honk on a blade of grass? Okay: your kids will love it. Or maybe your doctor will tell you it's good for your blood pressure or something. I don't know. Just try it—it'll make you happy.

John Javna

JUMPING ROPE

Background

People have been jumping rope for at least 400 years—although they haven't always used rope. In Sweden, "stiff wicker" was used. Cherokee Indians used grapevines. And Spanish children used strips of rubber.

•One 19th century English historian wrote: "In the hop season, a hop-stem stripped of its leaves is used instead of a rope, and in my opinion is preferable."

•Rhymes have been a part of jumping rope since the late 1800s, when city kids adapted the pastime as a group activity, with two people turning the rope while another jumped over it.

•There are over 2,500 different jump rope rhymes on record.

You'll Need:

A rope

You've got two options:

1. A jump rope with handles can be purchased at a sporting goods store.

2. You can make your own jump rope out of sash cord (which you can buy by the foot at most hardware stores). Either #7 or #10 cord will do. And any material is fine—cotton, nylon, polyethylene.

Proper Jump Rope Length:
When you stand on the cord, the ends of the rope should reach to your armpits.

BEGINNERS' TIPS

Before You Jump

- Do some warm-up excercises.
- Put on the right shoes—either aerobic or running shoes, because they absorb the impact when you jump.
- It's fun, but jumping rope is still pretty strenuous. Don't overdo it.
- Start slow, and work your way up to full speed over the course of several weeks.
- Try out each new bit of footwork without the rope first.

Technique

- Your elbows should be close to your body, with your hands extended about a foot from your sides.

- Keep your wrists loose. Beginners tend to turn the rope with their arms, but it's your fingers and wrists that should do the turning.
- Bounce as you jump.
- Land on the balls of your feet most of the time; occasionally land on your heels to keep your legs stretched out.
- Start out with the rope in back of you, at your feet.
- You only need to jump about an inch off the ground.
- Land in the same spot each time.

7

BASIC JUMPS

Notes

Before you can do the tricks, you've got to know the 3 basic jumps:
- The 2-foot jump
- The 2-foot jump with a bounce
- The skipping jump

You probably already know these. But I've included them anyway, just in case.

Technique:

•Start with the rope in back of you, at your feet, and bring it forward, over your head.

Variation: Try it backward, turning the rope from front to back instead of from back to front. It's a little harder.

2-Foot Jump

Jump once with your feet together each time the rope passes under you.

2-Foot Jump with a Bounce

Add a slight bounce after you jump over the rope.

Skipping Jump

Jump rope 1 foot at a time, stepping over it (or running in place over it).

KICKS

Notes

This looks and feels a little like tap dancing when you get it right.
There are lots of variations to experiment with. Remember: both feet land at the same time.

TIPS:

If this is too hard, insert a 2-foot jump between kicks. The formula is:
• 2-foot jump
• Jump and extend foot, touch heel
• 2-foot jump
• Jump and extend foot, etc.

If that's too easy, try touching your toe in back of you after each kick (with a jump for each move).

Instructions

1. Jump with your feet together.

2. On the next jump, land with your right foot out in front of you, touching your heel to the floor. Weight is on your left foot.

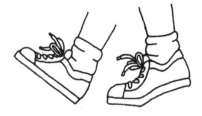

3. On the next jump, reverse the position and land with your left foot in

front, heel touching the floor. Weight is on your right foot.

CROSSING JUMP

Notes

This is the trick you always see boxers doing. When you get it right, it feels as slick as it looks.

TIPS:

It's a good idea to start working on the arm motion for this trick without the rope. You can also try out the arm motion with the rope, but *without* jumping.

• The most important thing is to make the loop in the rope big enough to jump through. Do that by crossing your arms at the elbows and pointing your hands straight out, away from your sides.

Instructions

1. Do a normal 2-foot jump.

2. On the next turn:
• As the rope comes down over your head, cross your arms at the elbows, pointing hands straight out.
• Rope will continue downward.
• Jump over the rope with hands in crossed postion.

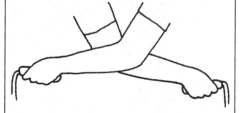

3. Arms are still in crossed position. The rope will continue over your head.

4. As the rope comes down over your head, separate your arms and do a normal 2-foot jump.

5. Keep going.

THE TWIST

Notes

This is the jump rope equivalent of a ballet move. You cross 1 foot over the other while you're in the air and then, on the next jump, reverse them.

TIPS:

• If this is too hard, simplify it by putting a 2-foot jump between leg crossings. The E-Z formula:
• 2-foot jump
• Cross right foot over left
• 2-foot jump
• Cross left foot over right, etc.

Another variation: Put a bounce into each jump and cross your legs on each jump, uncross them on each bounce.

Instructions

1. Do a regular 2-foot jump.

2. On the next jump, cross your right leg over your left at the ankles. Land on the balls of your feet, with your weight on your left foot.

3. Next jump: Cross your left leg over your right. Land on the balls of your feet, with your weight on your right foot.

4. Keep going.

Note: This move can be combined with the heel-toe variation of Kicks.

TWIST & TURN

Notes

This is a variation of the Twist. You cross 1 leg over and then turn all the way around in that position while you jump. It was devised as part of a fitness program.

TIPS:

• Again, if you find this too hard, simplify it by putting a regular 2-foot jump between jumps with the legs crossed. The E-Z formula:
•2-foot jump
•Cross right foot over left and jump
•Repeat

Another variation: Put a bounce into each jump; cross your legs on each jump and uncross them on each bounce.

Instructions

1. Do a regular 2-foot jump.

2. On the next jump, cross your right leg over your left at the ankles. Land on the balls of your feet, with your weight on your left foot.

3. Next jump: Begin turning to your left. Keep turning with each jump until you're back where you started. (It should take around 4 or 5 jumps.)

If you're ambitious: Without stopping, cross your left leg over and turn to your right. You can keep going like this until you're too dizzy to continue.

DOUBLE JUMP

Notes

This is the macho jump for people who want to challenge themselves physically, swinging the rope twice on 1 jump. Obviously, this takes practice. The world record, by the way, is 5 turns on 1 jump.

Instructions

1. Do a few 2-foot jumps.

2. On the next turn, jump as high as you can, pointing your toes. Whip the rope around as fast as possible.

PLAYGROUND JUMPING

Notes

This requires at least 3 people (or 2 people and a tree or fence to tie the rope to). Two (called "enders") turn the rope while a third jumps.
•A longer jump rope is necessary—an old clothesline works pretty well.
•When the rope is being swung toward the jumper, it's called "front door." When it's swung away from the jumper, it's called "back door."

TIPS:

It's tough to get in when you're first starting, but keep trying—you'll get it.
•The jumper should stay close to the center of the rope and try to land in the same spot throughout.

Instructions

1. The enders begin turning the rope, keeping it at a reasonable speed (not too fast).

2. The jumper stands outside the rope's arc until she or he is ready. Then she or he steps into place and begins jumping.

Tip for getting in:
•Stand as close to the rope as possible (without letting it hit you). The second it goes past you, go to the place where it touched the ground. Now wait for it to come around again. Start jumping.

DOUBLE DUTCH

Notes

Once you can do a 3-person jump with a single rope, move on to the super-tough old standard, Double Dutch—jumping 2 ropes at once.

TIPS:

Even being an ender in Double Dutch isn't easy. Some pointers:
• Turn both ropes inward.
• Set up a rhythm, so you're alternating evenly between the ropes.
• Hold 1 rope a little higher than the other.
• Turn the lower rope first.
• Once the lower 1 is turning smoothly, add in the higher rope.

Instructions

1. Enders begin turning the ropes in opposite directions, alternating evenly between them.

2. Jumper waits until the right moment (good luck) and runs in. Jumper then has to keep hopping over ropes coming from each direction.

Hint: Beginners should do 2-foot jumps, moving from side to side over the ropes.

JUMPING RHYMES

1. Cinderella,
dressed in yella,
went upstairs
to meet her fella.
On her way her girdle busted.
How many people
were disgusted?
1, 2, 3, 4...

2. Down by the meadow
where the green grass grows,
there stood (girl's name),
pretty as a rose.
Along came (boy's name),
and he sang so sweet.
He leaned over,
And he kissed her on the cheek.
How many kisses did she get?
1, 2, 3, 4...

3. I'm a little Dutch girl,
dressed in blue.
Here are the things
that I like to do:
Salute to the captain,
curtsey to the queen,
and hit them both
with a rotten tangerine.

4. Teddy Bear, Teddy Bear,
turn around.
Teddy Bear, Teddy Bear,
touch the ground.
Teddy Bear, Teddy Bear,
shine your shoe.
Teddy Bear, Teddy Bear,
how old are you?
1, 2, 3, 4...

5. Johnny on the ocean,
Johnny on the sea.
Johnny broke a bottle,
and he blamed it on me.
I told Ma,
Ma told Pa,
and Johnny got a lickin',
ha-ha-ha.
How many lickin's did he get?
1, 2, 3, 4...

6. (Boy's name) and (girl's name),
sitting in a tree, K-I-S-S-I-N-G.
First comes love,
then comes marriage,
then comes (girl's name)
with a baby carriage.
How many babies did she have?
1, 2, 3, 4...

CARD TRICKS

Background

•Playing cards originated in the Far East—China or India. They were introduced to Europe around A.D. 1100 by Crusaders who'd seen Arabs playing card games in the Holy Land. .

•Originally, each suit in European playing cards represented a social group. Noblemen were swords (which became spades); the clergy were cups (which became hearts); the merchant class was coins (which became diamonds); and the peasants were staves (which became clubs).

•Card tricks are believed to have originated in the 16th century, created by magicians entertaining royalty.

• The tricks in this section are the "automatic" kind—there's no sleight of hand or fancy dealing. They work mathematically, so anyone can do them.

You'll Need:

A clean deck of 52 playing cards
• Jokers aren't used in the tricks.

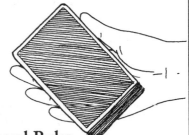

General Rules

• Keep your audience distracted with a running commentary—what you say is as important as what you do with the cards.

• Get your audience to trust you. (Make them believe there is "nothing up your sleeve," and that kind of stuff.)

•Start each trick by shuffling the cards and having someone from your audience cut the deck.

SWEET 15

Notes

This is an easy, almost foolproof trick.
• All you have to do is make sure the cards are stacked and dealt correctly at the beginning or end of each step.
• You don't even handle the cards in this one—a volunteer from the audience does all the work.

Instructions

1. Your volunteer shuffles the deck.

2. Ask the volunteer to deal out 15 cards on the table, placing 3 cards across, face down, 5 times. Set aside the rest of the deck.

3. Ask the volunteer to pick up 1 pile and remember 1 card. Instruct the volunteer to shuffle that pile and place it on top of 1 of the other piles on the table.

4. Place the remaining pile of 5 cards on top so that *your volunteer's pile is in the middle of the 3 original piles.*

5. Now hand your volunteer the pile of 15 cards again. Have the volunteer deal 5 cards across, 3 times.
• There will be 5 piles with 3 cards in each pile. Cards are face down.

6. Turn over all 5 piles so the bottom cards show.

7. Ask your volunteer to look through each pile and tell you which pile contains his or her card.

8. If you do it right, your volunteer's card will always be the one in the middle of that pile.

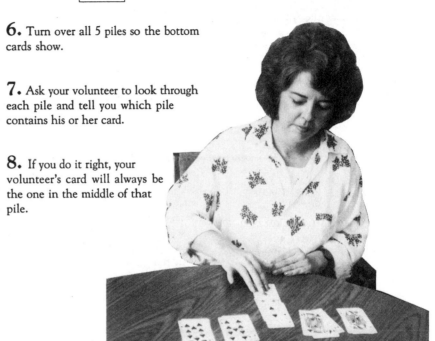

19

TIME-WISE

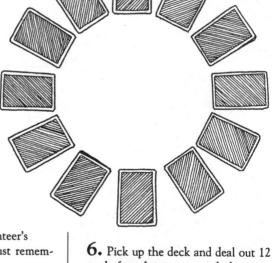

Notes

• In this trick, you find your volunteer's "secret card" by laying out cards in a circle that represents the face of a clock.

Instructions

1. Have a volunteer shuffle the deck.

2. Slide the top 13 cards off the deck. (Do it surreptitiously—don't let the audience know you're counting.)

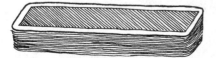

3. Give the 13 cards to the volunteer.

4. Tell your volunteer that you'll look away while he or she takes a few of the cards and puts them someplace where you won't see them. When that's done, tell him or her to shuffle the remaining cards and look at the bottom one. That's the volunteer's "secret" card—he or she must remember it.

5. The volunteer puts the remaining pile of cards back on top of the deck.

6. Pick up the deck and deal out 12 cards face down, *counterclockwise* in circle. The first card is at 12 o'clock, the second card is at 11 o'clock, the third is at 10 o'clock, etc.

7. Point out to your audience that this circle is like the face of a clock. Ramble on about where each "hour" is ("This card is 5 o'clock," etc.).

• The fact that it's a clock really has nothing to do with the trick. This is intended only to entertain and distract your audience and to give the trick a context.

8. Now put the rest of the deck aside.

• Ask your volunteer to uncover the cards he or she has set aside and count them out. Explain that the number of cards the volunteer has taken is the "hour" at which his or her "secret card" will appear. (Let's say there are 6 cards—then the secret card is in the 6 o'clock position, etc.)

9. Tell your volunteer to announce his or her "secret card." Then, with great drama, flip over the correct card. It will work every time.

3 AT ONCE

Notes

This is a really amazing trick.
• For maximum effect, you need 3 helpers—though you *can* do it with 1.
• You need a full 52-card deck—no jokers, no cards missing.

Instructions

1. Assuming you're using 3 helpers: Have each helper take a card from the deck. Tell each of them to remember his or her "secret card."

2. Be glib; keep talking to your audience as you slide 15 cards off the top of the deck.
• Pull out the cards by groups of 5 in

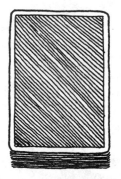
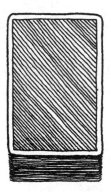
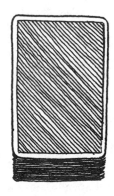

an offhand manner. No one should notice you're counting.

3. Place the 15 cards in a stack in front of you, on the right.

4. Take another 15 cards and put

them on the table to the left of the first stack.

5. Take 10 more cards and put them to the left of the last stack (see illustration). You should have 9 cards left in your hand.

6. Have helper #1 pick up the stack of cards at the far left (the one with 10 cards in it) and shuffle it.
• Tell him to put his card on top.

7. Now have helper #1 take some cards from the middle stack and shuffle them.
•Tell the helper to put them on top of his card. It's now "buried."

8. Helper #2 shuffles the middle stack and puts his card on top of it.

9. Have helper #3 take a few cards from the far right pile and put them on top of helper #2's card in the middle pile. Now that card is "buried," too.

10. The third helper goes through the same routine, shuffling the stack on the far right and putting his card on top of it. Give him or her your 9 cards to shuffle and put them on top of that pile. Helper #3's card is now "buried," too.

11. Pick up the 3 stacks from right to left. The far right pile will be on top, the middle pile in the middle, and the far left pile on the bottom.

12. You're now holding the full deck. Take 4 cards off the top and put them on the bottom of the deck as you tell everyone that your helpers' cards are hopelessly lost.

13. Tell your audience that you'll be dealing out the cards in 2 stacks—one with cards face up, one with cards face down. Tell each helper that when his card turns up, he should yell "Stop!"

14. Deal the first card face up; the next one face down. Then another in the "face up" pile; another face down. Keep doing this until you're out of cards. (No one will say "Stop.")
• Act surprised that none of the helpers' cards has appeared (heh, heh).

15. Discard the entire "face up" pile. You don't need it anymore.

16. Repeat the face up, face down process, using *only* the "face down" pile each time.
• Discard the "face up" pile each time.
• Always start with a "face up" card.
• Keep doing this until you have only 3 cards left. They are all face down.

17. Leaving the cards face down, hand the top card to helper #3, the middle card to helper #2, and the bottom card to helper #1.
• Ask the helpers to tell you what their secret cards were—and after each one does, tell him or her to turn over the card he or she is holding. Each one will be holding his or her original card. It's astounding!

4 DOWN

Notes

Use a 52-card deck. No jokers.

Instructions

1. Ask your volunteer to shuffle the deck and cut it exactly in half. Get as close as you can on this one. (Put both halves side by side on the table. This will help you judge the evenness of the cut.)
• If the split is too far off, this trick will not work.

2. Have your volunteer take a card from the middle of one of the piles, remember it, and put it on *top* of that half of the deck.

3. Place the other half of the deck on top of the selected card. The card is now "buried" in the deck.

4. Ask your volunteer to deal the whole deck into 4 piles, starting with the top card. The volunteer must deal the cards one at a time, left to right.

5. Now turn each pile over so the faces of the cards show.

6. Ask your volunteer to point to the pile containing the selected card.

7. Turn that pile face down. Set the other piles aside.

8. Give the "face down" pile to your volunteer. Ask the volunteer to deal out 4 more piles, face down.

9. The last card he or she deals will fall on the first pile. Since it now contains an "uneven" amount of cards, throw that pile away.

10. Take the top and bottom cards of each of the remaining 3 piles and throw them away. Now you've got 3 cards left.

11. Pick the cards up from left to right and give them to your volunteer, face down.
• Tell your volunteer to discard the **top** and bottom cards.
• The card that's left will be your volunteer's card.

BOOMERANGS

Background

The Australian natives of New South Wales, who used the boomerang mainly for hunting, are the people most closely identified with it. However, other cultures around the world have used similar devices for war and hunting. Among them: the ancient Egyptians, natives of southern India, and the Hopi Indians of North America.

• Birds are actually attracted to flying boomerangs, rather than being frightened of them, so birds are a favorite hunting target.

• Besides the familiar Australian Bushman model, there are 3 other types of boomerangs:

   1. The Cross-stick boomerang, made from 2 sticks fastened together.

   2. The Boomabird, a boomerang constructed to look like a bird.

   3. The Tumblestick, a straight stick designed to return to the thrower.

They can all be made of cardboard, and all 3 work remarkably well.

You'll Need:

Cardboard
Rather than dealing with full-size wooden boomerangs, we'll make a few cardboard versions.

•You can use almost any kind of cardboard *except* corrugated.

•Good sources: cardboard from the back of a pad of paper, packing from laundered shirts, etc.

•The heavier the cardboard is, the bigger the boomerang can be.

Pen or Pencil

Scissors

BEGINNERS' TIPS

How to Throw Them

It takes no skill to throw boomerangs —just a little practice and technique.

It's an unexplained phenomenon that boomerangs can be thrown only from right to left. So if you're left-handed, you should try throwing with your right hand.

•If you have to throw left-handed, throw the boomerang so it curves to the left, not to the right.

•It's all in the wrist and angle.

Instructions

1. Hold the boomerang between your thumb and first finger, perpendicular to the ground.

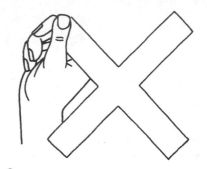

2. Bring your wrist and arm straight back, alongside your ears, keeping the boomerang perpendicular to the ground.

3. Snap your wrist forward and release. That's all there is to it.

CROSS-STICK BOOMERANG

Notes

To make this, all you need is an 8-1/2" square piece of cardboard. Remember that you can use almost any kind of cardboard *except* corrugated.

Instructions

1. Mark out a cross on your cardboard. The wings should be 8-1/2" long and 1" wide, as shown in the diagram. Cut out the design with your scissors.

2. Bend the end of each of the 4 wings slightly upward. About 2" from the end will do the trick. Don't go overboard and crease the cardboard. You just want a nice, subtle curve.

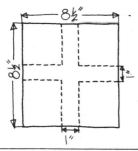

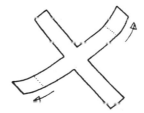

3. Throw the boomerang according to the instructions in "Beginners' Tips."
• Watch the boomerang sail forward, turn to the left, and go higher in the air. It will then flatten horizontally and glide back to you.

CARDBOARD BOOMABIRD

Notes

The Boomabird is an unusual type of boomerang that's traditionally decorated to look like a bird. Again, you can make one out of almost any kind of cardboard except corrugated.

You'll Need:
- Scissors
- An 8-1/2" x 9" piece of cardboard.

Instructions

1. To Make the Boomabird:

Mark out the drawing of the Boomabird according to the diagram. The wings should be 8-1/2" long, and the body should be 9" long. The wings

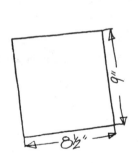

should be 1" wide but rounded at each end. The bird's body should taper according to the diagram. Cut out the Boomabird with your scissors.

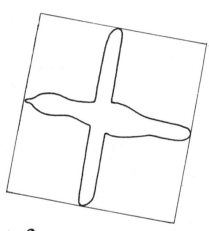

2. Bend the ends of both wings and both ends of the body slightly upward as with the Cross-stick, about 2" from the end. Don't crease them.

To Throw the Boomabird

1. Follow the directions under "Beginners' Tips."

•Hold the end of a Boomabird wing between your first finger and thumb, perpendicular to the ground.

2. Cock your arm and wrist, then snap your wrist forward and release.

3. The Boomabird's flight pattern is different from the Cross-stick's.

•After you throw it, you'll notice it goes straight forward, swings to the left, and rises in the air.

•It then makes a circle over you, goes around in front, reverses direction, and returns to you.

Decorating the Boomabird

• Paint or color the body and the wings of your Boomabird in a solid tone and then outline it with a contrasting color so you can see it better when it's in flight.

• Consider other designs, such as a Boomafish. (You've never heard of a flying fish?) Or a Boomaplane. Remember: keep the proportions the same as for the Boomabird.

THE TUMBLESTICK

Notes

This is simply amazing. A Tumblestick is a regular, straight piece of cardboard that, when hurled into the air, actually returns to you. Don't ask me to explain it—I wouldn't believe it myself if I hadn't tried it.

• You'll need 1 piece of cardboard 8-1/2" long and up to 2" wide.

TIPS:

• Throwing a Tumblestick is all in the wrist and angle.

• Be careful not to bend the cardboard. Unlike other boomerangs, this one needs to be flat.

• Narrower Tumblesticks will rotate faster when thrown.

Instructions

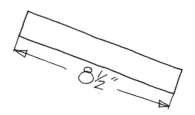

8½"

1. Cut out a Tumblestick

• You can make a Tumblestick in any of the following widths: 1-7/8", 1-1/2", 1-3/8", or 1". For some reason, other widths don't seem to work.

• Always make it 8-1/2" long.

• Grab the Tumblestick between your first finger and thumb. Hold it perpendicular to the ground, just over your right ear.

• Snap your wrist forward and release it upward at a 45-degree angle.

• Watch the Tumblestick sail up, curve to the left, and then tumble back toward you horizontally. It always returns!

RESTAURANT TRICKS

Background

•The first restaurant known to archae-ologists was in ancient Egypt. Ruins indicate that it was long and narrow, had a counter and stools, and even had a primitive version of the modern grill. It's not known whether they fixed burgers there, but french fries certainly hadn't been invented yet.

•Nowadays, restaurants are a multi-billion dollar business.

•Besides traffic jams, we probably spend more time waiting in restau-rants than anywhere.

•Naturally, we look for ways to amuse ourselves. So when you've fin-ished with the connect-the-dots place mats and the free coloring books, you can turn to time-tested tricks like these.

You'll Need:

Tableware
If you go to the same kind of restau-rants I do, you'll find everything you need for these tricks on the table or the front counter—silverware, water, napkins, matches, glasses, toothpicks, salt, and sugar.

FLOATING SILVERWARE

Notes

This is easy, but it looks impossible. Using only a toothpick, you can balance a fork and spoon on the edge of a water glass.

•Then you can set the toothpick on fire. When it burns down, it leaves only a small piece of wood balancing the silverware.

You'll Need:

•A spoon and a fork
•A toothpick (flat or round)
•Matches
•A water glass

Instructions

1. Connect the spoon and fork by placing the edge of the spoon between the fork's tines.

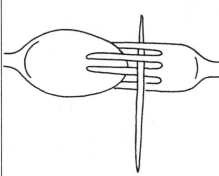

2. Stick a toothpick in the middle space of the fork. Center it.

3. Place the other end of the tooth-pick on the rim of the glass and find the balancing point.
•The toothpick/silverware apparatus will balance on the edge of the glass—a great trick in itself.

4. Using a match, carefully light a fire at both ends of the toothpick.
•The ends will burn down until they reach the glass and silverware.
•Gently blow away any remaining ashes.

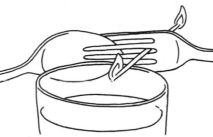

5. What's left seems impossible. The toothpick/silverware apparatus will appear ready to topple off the glass, but for some reason it doesn't. In fact, you can lightly tap it (and pick up and set down the glass), and it will remain balanced. Incredible.

HANGING SPOONS

Notes

While you're waiting for your food, you can always hang a spoon on your nose.

• This is a particularly enjoyable group activity. There's nothing more aesthetically pleasing than a table full of people with spoons hanging from their faces.

• Believe it or not, there's a whole book about this subject. It's called *How to Hang a Spoon*, by Joe Martin.

TIPS:

• The spoon must be warm.

• Warm it up by placing it in your mouth (without touching your lips or tongue). Breathe on it until it fogs up.

Hang the Spoon from Your Nose

1. Hold the handle of the spoon and tilt your head back.

2. Place the spoon on your nose.

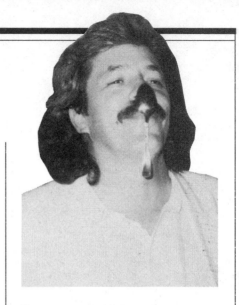

3. Pull the spoon gently forward until you feel it "catch."

4. Gently move your head forward until it's upright.

Hang the Spoon on Your Face

1. Lay the spoon against your face, gently keeping it in place with your first finger.

2. Concentrate on a point in front of you, at eye level.

3. Let go. The spoon will hang on your face.

THE DRIPLESS GLASS

Notes

This is a classic. It's not actually dripless, but it probably won't spill all over your table. Well, actually, if you do it wrong, it probably will... but that's a chance you'll have to take.

•It's simple: You place a paper napkin over a filled water glass, flip it over, and the water stays in the glass.

•I recommend that you perfect this over a kitchen sink. I also recommend that you do it over a bowl, so if you flub up it doesn't soak everyone at your table.

Instructions

1. Place a glass filled to the top with water in front of you.

2. Place a napkin over the top of the glass, folding the ends of the napkin over the sides of the glass.

3. Holding on to the ends of the napkin, turn the glass over. The napkin will soak through.

4. When the part of the napkin on the side of the glass is wet, you can let go of the napkin. A little water may drip through the paper, but the napkin will stay in place for a short while.

WHAT NOW?

Notes

This probably falls into the category of *dirty* trick rather than cool trick, but what the hell.
•You'll need 2 filled water glasses.

Instructions

1. Tell a companion that you've got a good trick to demonstrate.

2. Give these instructions: "Put your hands out in front of you on the table, palms down. First, I'll balance these water glasses on the back of your hands."
•Carefully balance the glasses on the backs of your companion's hands.

3. What now? That's it; your companion is at your mercy. He or she can't do anything without spilling or breaking the glasses.

ICE ROUNDUP

Notes

You need a piece of string or thread for this, but if you didn't happen to bring one with you to the restaurant, use a hair.

• You also need a full water glass with an ice cube in it.

Instructions

1. If you're using a string or thread, take it out and tie a little loop at the end. Challenge anyone at your table to lift the ice cube with it.

• If you're using a hair, tell your companions that this particular hair is the strongest you've ever seen—so strong that you can lift an ice cube with it.

2. After everyone's tried to lift the ice (and failed), lay the string or hair over the ice cube.

• Pour some salt on it.

3. The salt will melt the ice cube, and the cold will freeze it again.

• The string or hair will be attached to the cube. Gently lift them both.

GIANT BUBBLES

Background

- People have been playing with bubbles for centuries.
- When Flemish artist Pieter Breughel the Elder chronicled children's play in his 1560 painting, *Children's Games*, he included a child blowing bubbles with a clay pipe. That's the earliest record of bubble-blowing.
- The dean of modern bubble-ology is Eiffel Plasterer, an Indiana professor who has managed to preserve a bubble in a jar for 340 days.
- Other modern bubble artists include Richard Faverty (aka Professor Bubbles), who developed the people-size bubble, and Tom Noddy, who specializes in smoke-filled bubbles.

You'll Need:

Bubble solution
The simplest way to get some is to buy a container of commercial solution. However, it's considerably more economical to make your own. I'll explain how on the following page.

- If you do make your own, you'll need dishwashing liquid—preferably *Joy* or *Dawn* because they contain a special ingredient that actually makes bubble walls stronger.

Glycerine
- Pure glycerine (not the kind with rose water in it) is available at any drugstore.
- It's a thickening agent that makes the bubble walls last longer.

And...
- A pair of pliers
- A wire coat hanger
- Cotton string
- A pan about 18" x 18"

And a few other things I'll get to later.

BEGINNERS' TIPS

Making Big Bubbles

It's really no harder to make big bubbles than small ones, but it's a hell of a lot more fun.

•Weather conditions will affect your bubble-making.

•On a still day, because there's no air turbulence, you can make huge bubbles.

•But when there's a breeze, it's harder to make big bubbles—the wind pops them. Instead, you can just hold your hoop up to the breeze and twist it back and forth like a weather vane. The wind will blow out batches of bubbles.

•When there's a gentle breeze, you can blow out long tubes of bubbles.

Note: Keep the foam out of your bubble solution. After you use it awhile, your pan of bubble solution will get foamy on top. Most people don't realize that this is bad for bubble-making. The foam creates little bubbles in the solution that pop bigger bubbles.

•Periodically scrape the foam off with a piece of cardboard.

Make Your Own Solution

This is fairly easy, although you'll have to experiment to get it just right.

The formula is:

5 cups water
1/2 cup dishwashing liquid
1/8 cup glycerine

Change it proportionately to fit your needs.

The material in this chapter is taken from *The Official Bubble Handbook*, by Professor Bubbles. It is by far the most complete book on bubble activities ever written. If you'd like information about it, write to:

Bubbles
Box 25
1400 Shattuck Avenue
Berkeley, CA 94709

COAT HANGER HOOPS

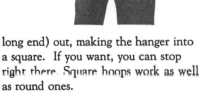

Notes

These homemade hoops are great. Even though they're just constructed of coat hangers, they'll give you 3- or 4-foot bubbles every time.

You'll Need:

- A wire coat hanger
- A pair of pliers
- Some cotton string

After you make the hoop, you'll need:
- Lots of bubble solution
- A pan wide and deep enough to immerse the hoop in. (A large aluminum baking pan works well, but any cooking pan will do, as long as you can lay the hoop flat into the pan.)

Instructions

1. With the pliers, bend the hooked end of the coat hanger so it's flat. This will be the hoop's handle.

2. Hold on to the top of the hanger (the handle) and pull the bottom (the long end) out, making the hanger into a square. If you want, you can stop right there. Square hoops work as well as round ones.

- If you want to make your hoop round, bend the sides all the way around and form them into a circle (or as close as you can get).

3. Cut off a length of cotton string about 3 feet long. Tie 1 end of the string onto the handle and begin wrapping it around the hoop.

• The string is important; it holds the extra bubble solution needed to make the big bubbles.

• The string doesn't have to be wound supertight, but don't leave it hanging too loosely either.

4. When you get back around to the handle:

• Keep wrapping all the way up and down the handle until you run out of string.

• If you prefer, just cut off another piece of string and wrap the handle separately.

• It's important to get the handle wrapped well, because the wire will get too slippery by itself; string makes the handle easy to hold.

• Cut off any excess string.

TIPS:

• Make sure your hoop is as flat as possible.

• If you bend the handle up, the hoop becomes easier to dip into the bubble solution.

• The spot that most people miss when they're wrapping the coat hanger is the Y at the base of the handle. Be sure to fill that Y so no exposed wire is left there.

• If you don't get spectacular bubbles with your hoop, try wrapping a second length of string around the hoop in the opposite direction (making Xs with the first length).

Dipping the Hoop

Place the hoop flat into the pan and leave it there for a few seconds, until the string is soaked through.

•If you need to, force the hoop down gently into the solution with 1 hand.

•**Note:** Most people slosh their hoops around in the bubble solution to get them wet. That's unnecessary.
It just creates foam.

Lifting the Hoop Out of the Pan

If you pull the hoop straight out of the bubble solution, the bubble film will break with annoying regularity.

•The right way: turn the hoop on its side, perpendicular to the tray, while it's still in the solution.

•Gently lift it that way, and the bubble film will remain intact, without creating excess foam.

Make Gigantic Bubbles

1. Dip your hoop into the solution and get a bubble film across it.

2. Wave your hoop into the air, making a tube. When the tube gets to be about 3 feet long, gently twist your wrist so you're twisting off the end of the bubble.

•Slow, gentle movements are best. Swinging the hoop too fast breaks the bubble film.

• Start with smaller bubbles and work your way up to bigger ones.

Make a Bubble Sculpture

By dividing the opening of the hoop with string, you can create bubbles with many chambers and surfaces. As they float into the sky, they will take on all kinds of shapes and reflect light dramatically.

The artistry of this trick is in the designs you use to divide the bubble hoop. You can make any shapes and sizes on the frame—5 openings, 10 openings, a star, a square...use your imagination and experiment.

An example:

The "quadri-bubble"—a bubble with 4 openings.

1. Tie a piece of cotton string to 1 side of your hoop. Stretch it across the opening and tie it to the other side. Now you can make a bubble with 2 chambers.

2. Divide that again, making a cross across the hoop. Now you can make a 4-chamber bubble.

Walter, my next-door neighbor, demonstrates the quadri-bubble.

GIANT BUBBLE HOOPS

Notes

Now you can build giant hoops that will produce bubbles 8 to 10 feet in diameter. The principle of the big bubble hoop is the same as the coat hanger hoop—except that the wire has to be thicker, it's much harder to bend, and you need a much larger pan.... Plus, you need to mix up a lot more bubble solution.

You'll Need:

• 1/8"-thick aluminum or steel wire (It's available in 25- to 50-foot lengths at hardware stores.)
• A pair of pliers
• Cotton string—thicker and heavier than you used with the coat hanger

Instructions

1. Form a length of wire into a 3-foot-diameter circle.

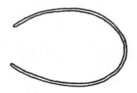

2. On each end, bend up about 9" of wire with a pair of pliers. That's the handle.

3. Using the string, lash these 2 halves of the handle together and wrap them the same way you did with the handle of the coat hanger hoop. Then tie them off.

4. Two inches up the handle, bend it back almost 90 degrees. Now the handle looks a little like a frying pan

handle—which makes it easier to dip.

5. Wrap the hoop with string the same way you wrapped the coat hanger—going back and forth about 4 times. Remember: the more you wrap

the hoop, the bigger your bubbles will be.

6. Dip your hoop in the solution the same way you dipped your coat hanger hoop, taking extra care when you lift and wave it. The huge expanse of bubble film will break quite easily. **Note:** You can make more hoops as large as you want, but they're pretty hard to handle when they're over 4

feet in diameter.

What Should You Use for a Pan?

I use a plastic, inflatable swimming pool that I bought at a toy store for under $10. You can imagine how much bubble solution it takes; however, you don't need to fill it all the way—just make it deep enough to immerse the hoop.

49

PAPER TRICKS

Background

American paper tricks include everything from grade school games to gimmicks with dollar bills. However, paper folding is an ancient art as well as entertainment.

• In Japan, it is called *origami* (*ori* means folding, and *gami* means paper). Using no glue, tape, or scissors, origami artists create representations of animals: delicate birds, lions, deer, frogs, etc. And occasionally, origami forms are practical. Hats, boats that float, and even a paper ball are part of Japanese tradition.

• In the West, Harry Houdini wrote the first book on paper magic. A few of his creations are included here.

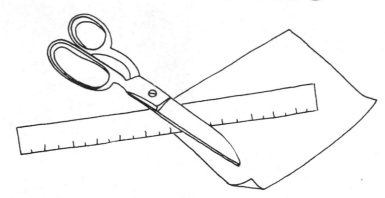

You'll Need:

Sheets of 8-1/2" X 11" paper

Many paper-folding tricks are done with square sheets of paper.

• There is a special origami paper— lightweight, colored, square—but you really don't need it for most of these projects.

• You will, however, need a pair of scissors (and maybe a ruler) to turn regular 8-1/2" X 11" sheets of paper into squares.

BEGINNERS' TIPS

Make It Square

A trick for turning a rectangular piece of writing paper into a square:

1. Fold 1 corner of the paper over so it is even with the edge, as shown.

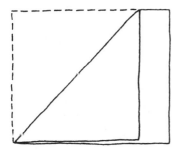

2. Draw a line along the edge of the resulting triangle. Fold along the line.

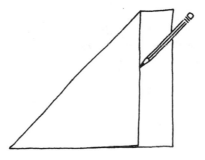

3. Unfold the triangle. Cut (or tear) along the line. You now have a square.

Note: When you fold paper, don't worry about getting the corners and lines to match up exactly—it rarely happens. Just try to make the folds as neatly and accurately as possible.

DOLLAR BOW TIE

Notes

A few folds, and you can make a bow tie out of a dollar bill. This is guaranteed to delight almost anyone, because it actually turns money into an article of clothing.

Instructions

1. Lay a dollar in front of you, with George Washington facing down. Fold the bill in half lengthwise to get a crease down the middle. Now unfold it.

2. Fold all 4 corners in to meet at the crease.

3. Fold the long edges of the paper in to meet at the crease.

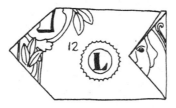

4. Fold the bill in half the short way. The smooth surface is on the outside.

5. Push the square corners in, folding them down the center so they're inverted inside the paper.

6. Fold the triangle at the closed end over.

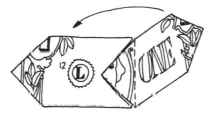

7. Open up the back flap, bringing it forward and around so it now covers the front flap (and hides the folded triangle inside).

8. There are four corners on the straight-edged side. Fold the corners on each side over so they meet at the center.
Note: They won't actually fold over neatly. But do the best you can.

9. Open the paper gently. You can see the "knot" with George's face on it. Keeping your fingers on the folds in the back, open the paper the rest of the way and flatten George's face so it's neat. That's it.

A paper clip will attach it to your shirt.

NEWSPAPER TREE

Notes

Remember watching a magician roll up a newspaper and turn it into a tree when you were a kid? It's your turn.

TIPS:

• When you roll up the **newspaper,** get it fairly tight.

• A single page of newspaper is easier to work with than a whole 2-page sheet. Begin with that.

• To make a huge tree: use 3 or 4 sheets of newspaper. Roll them up together and use a rubber band to keep the cylinder from unrolling while you work with it. Twist the paper to tighten it as you pull it out.

Instructions

1. Tear off a page from a newspaper.

2. Lay it down and roll it into a tight cylinder.

3. Make 3 vertical cuts in the cylinder, about halfway down. Space them evenly so the cylinder is cut into thirds.

4. Pull out the center, and you have an instant tree.

PAPER POPPER

Notes

If you fold the paper right, you can make a device that gives off a loud bang. In elementary school, everyone knew how to make these. Now there's no teacher to take them away from us, and we can make as much noise as we want.

Instructions

1. Fold an 8-1/2" x 11" sheet of paper in half lengthwise *and* widthwise. Now unfold it.

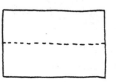

2. Fold the 4 corners in to meet the longer crease.

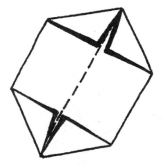

3. Fold the sheet of paper over, along the longer crease.

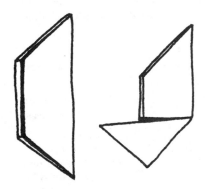

4. Fold the bottom corner up to meet the center line.

5. Fold the top corner down so it's sitting next to the bottom corner.

6. Fold the whole unit in half as shown.

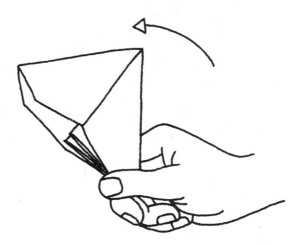

7. Grasp the paper between your thumb and first finger and snap it downward. The result should be a loud bang.

ELASTIC PAPER

Notes

This simple trick can be used in a bunch of different ways—from the silly to the surprising.

• You will fold a piece of paper in half and make cuts in it, alternating between top and bottom.

• Then watch it stretch. With a standard 8-1/2" x 11" piece of paper, you'll have a hole big enough to step through. With a smaller piece, you'll have an instant hat.

TIP:

• Try it with a playing **card, betting** that you can cut a hole in **the card** big enough to put your arm through. Depending on how big you are, you actually might be able to *walk* through it.

Instructions

1. Fold a sheet of paper lengthwise, then unfold and make a slit along the middle part of the line. Don't cut all the way to the edges of the paper.

2. Fold the paper in half lengthwise again.

3. Using scissors, make alternating cuts in the paper as shown.

• Cut in about 3/4 of the way.

• Make the cuts fairly close together.

Now you've got a silly hat...or a good way to win a few bets.

STRETCHING A BUCK

Notes

This is a variation of the Elastic Paper trick. Money tricks always get people's attention. Do it with fake money, of course.

Instructions

1. Fold a dollar bill in half lengthwise. Now unfold.

2. Fold the edges in to meet the crease.

3. Fold the dollar in half lengthwise, as shown.

4. Cut the bill as you did with the Elastic Paper, as shown. Cuts should be close together.

5. Put the bill in your wallet. In conversation, mention that you've learned how to stretch a buck better than anyone you know. Pull out the dollar and show your audience what you mean—then quickly put it back in your wallet so they can't examine it.

FORTUNE-TELLER

Notes

This is a forgotten grade school classic. It's also known as a Cootie Catcher or Cootie Picker.

Instructions

1. Start with a square sheet of paper. Fold the paper in half both ways. Then unfold it.

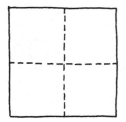

2. Fold all 4 corners in so they meet along the creases. Write the name of a different color on each triangle.

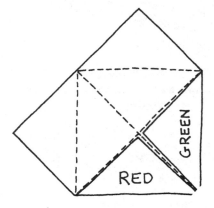

RED

GREEN

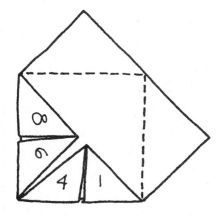

3. Turn the paper over. Fold all 4 corners in again. They meet the same way. Write a different number on each section of each triangle (8 total).

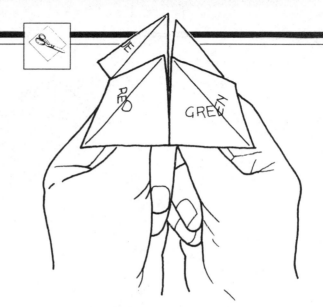

4. Now fold the paper in half so the colors are on the outside.

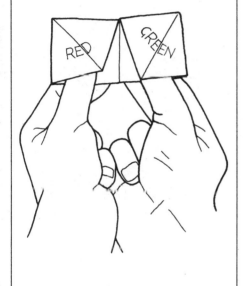

5. Insert your thumbs and first fingers into the flaps, and bend the Fortune-teller into shape, as shown.

6. Move the Fortune-teller by squeezing your fingers together.
• First, squeeze each thumb and first finger of the same hand together, opening the Fortune-teller out to the side.
• Next, squeeze the two thumbs and two first fingers together, opening the Fortune-teller up in the other direction.

7. Open the flaps under the numbers, and write a fortune under each section (8 in all). You can do it with a theme—e.g., "What will I be doing when I'm 50?" or with random ideas.

Sample Fortunes:

• You will become world-famous as the first person to design and build a condominium completely out of Twinkies.

• You will commit suicide by overdosing on "Gilligan's Island" reruns.

• You will be kidnapped by extraterrestrials who mistake you for Elvis's ghost.

• You will set a world record by playing the theme song from "Mr. Ed" backwards 56,784 times.

How You Play:

• Tell someone to pick one of the colors. Move the Fortune-teller in or out once for each letter.

• Then tell the person to pick a number. Move the Fortune-teller in and out that many times.

• Tell the person to pick one more number; that's the flap you open up to read the fortune.

JACKS

Background

- The game of jacks dates back to prehistoric times, when our ancestors played it using the wrist, knuckle, and ankle bones of animals as "jacks" (but without the ball, of course).
- There are actually cave drawings depicting the game.
- Pictures of the game also appear on ancient Greek urns, and references to it are found in histories of ancient Rome.
- Today, in many parts of the world, similar games are still played with primitive objects such as stones, straw, seeds, bones, and filled cloth bags.
- Jacks has been played in America for centuries, mostly by girls.

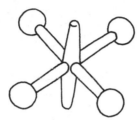

You'll Need:

A set of jacks (usually between 6 and 10)
- Plastic and metal jacks are available at almost any toy store.
- Metal ones are better because they're heavier and don't scatter as easily when you toss them.

- If you have small hands, it's better to start with lighter, thinner jacks.

A jack ball (about 1-1/4" in diameter)
- Ball test: Throw your ball straight up in the air. If it bounces back up at least half as high as it fell, it's a good one.

At *least* 3 square feet of quality playing surface
- The best surface to play on is a smooth, but not highly polished, floor. (Too much polish makes for runaway jacks.)
- Beware of floors with splinters or big cracks.

FLIPPING JACKS

Notes

This is how you begin every game of jacks to see who goes first and to determine where you start—but it's also a game in itself.

• You don't use a ball.

• You toss the jacks into the air, then try to catch them on the back of your hand. Then you flip them back the other way, trying to catch them in the palm of your hand again.

• Of course, you're going to drop a bunch of jacks in the process; the point is to drop fewer than your opponent.

• You can do it 2-handed (easier) or 1-handed (for experts).

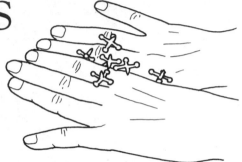

2-Handed Flipping

1. Pick up the jacks and cup your hands together; jiggle the jacks into a neat row or pile in the middle.

2. Throw the jacks straight up and catch them on the back of your hands (keeping thumbs together, fingers extended and bent up to form a sort of cradle).

3. Jiggle the jacks into the middle again. Toss them straight up, flip your hands over, and catch the jacks in your cupped hands. Your goal is to drop as few jacks as possible in the combined steps.

1-Handed Flips

This is virtually the same as 2-handed flips...except it's a lot harder—and you're going to drop more jacks.

The secret of catching jacks on one hand: Spread your fingers apart and trap the jacks between them. But don't spread your fingers so much that the jacks slip out.

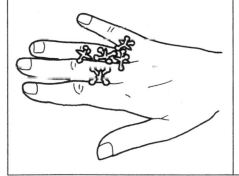

How to Use Flipping

As a trick:
• Flip once. Then, on the second flip—while the jacks are still in the air—try to pick up the jacks you dropped. Good luck.

To begin a game of jacks:
• All players flip front and back.
• Whoever drops the fewest jacks goes first.

BASIC JACKS (PLAINSIES)

Notes

If you played jacks as a kid, this is the game you remember best. You pick up the jacks 1 at a time, then 2 at a time, 3 at a time, and so on, until you scoop them all up in 1 handful. It sounds simple...but when you try to do it, you'll gain a new respect for how coordinated you once were.

TIPS:

• You have more control over the jacks if you throw them with the side of your hand touching the floor.
• Toss the ball as high as necessary to give yourself time. For close-together jacks, toss the ball higher.

Instructions

1. Flip to see who goes first.

2. Whoever wins the flipping repeats the process:
• If you flip and don't drop any jacks, you can skip onesies.
• Flip again; if you're successful again, skip twosies....And so forth, until you drop a jack.

3. Let's say you start at onesies (which is likely).
• Scatter the jacks on the floor.
• Throw the ball straight up, pick up 1 jack, and after the ball has bounced once, catch it in the same hand.

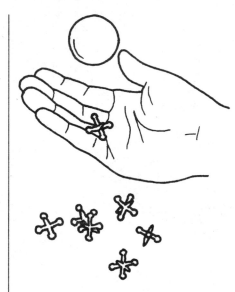

4. Now transfer the jack to your other hand and repeat the process, picking up one jack at a time until you either get all of them or miss.

5. If you catch them all, go on to twosies (same as onesies, except you have

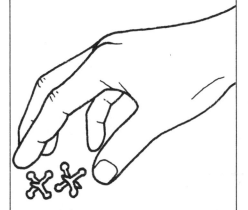

to pick up the jacks 2 at a time) and then to threesies.

6. After threesies:
When you get to foursies, you pick up 4 jacks, then 2.
• On fivesies, pick up 5 jacks, then 1.
• On sixsies, sweep them all up in 1 movement. If you're amazing enough to make it to twosies, or—unbelievably—sixsies, and you get a foul or miss (i.e., picking up the wrong number of jacks or touching jacks you're not trying to pick up), then you have to go back to onesies on your next turn and start again. Aggh!

SHADOW ANIMALS

Background

It's a safe guess that human beings have been creating shadow figures since they first noticed shadows. But the earliest record I can find is in a book called *Hand Shadows to Be Thrown Upon the Wall*, written by Henry Bursill. It was originally published in 1859.

• Bursill cites a picture entitled *The Rabbit on the Wall*, by a painter named Willkie, as the inspiration for his work.

• He also mentions that other books had previously been written on the subject of shadow animals. Unfortunately, they seem to be lost.

You'll Need:

Your hands

A focused light in a dark room
• The light should be shining directly

onto a wall, so if you use a lamp, either remove the shade or tilt it toward the wall.

• You'll want a crisp, sharp shadow, so select your light accordingly.

BEGINNERS' TIPS

Position

• Stand between the light and the wall, close enough to the wall so your shadows are clear and crisp.
• Stand sideways and extend your hands in front of you.
• If the light is too close to the wall, your shadows will be fuzzy.
• Experiment. Move the light as far from the wall as possible, then move it toward the wall until the shadows are just right.

Play the Angles

• The angle of your hand in relation to the wall will determine what is seen. (To experiment: keep your hand in the same position and try tilting it at the wrist. Watch the difference in the shadow.)

Left and Right

Most of these diagrams are drawn from a right-handed person's perspective. If you're left-handed, reverse them.

Be Aware of Your Arm

Unbuttoned sleeves or bulky sweaters can ruin the illusion. If clothing is in the way, push it back.

Eyes

This is the hardest part of an "animal" to get right, but worth working on. A well-placed, well-formed eye is often the only internal detail on a face, so it adds a lot to the illusion.

Exercises

Dedicated shadow artists do finger exercises to increase their finger mobility. If you're interested, you'll find some in the book *Shadowplay*, by George Mendoza.

SIMPLE FIGURES

A Weird Face

A Bird

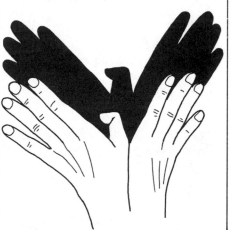

A Hawk

A 2-Handed Dog

Put your palms together, thumbs on top.
• Separate your thumbs so they look like ears.
• Lower 1 of your little fingers so it looks like a mouth. Move the ears and mouth to add realism.

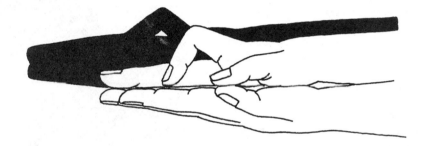

An Alligator

Use your whole arm for this.
• Hold your left arm out, with your left hand open and flat, palm up.
• Lay your right hand, palm down, on top of your left hand.

• Bend the right first finger, arching it until you have what appears to be a triangular bump with a hole in it. This is both the eye and the top of the alligator's head.
• Slowly open and close your hands to simulate a mouth.

AN ELEPHANT

Notes

This is from Henry Bursill's 1859 volume on shadow animals, which includes no text at all—just sketches, as shown here. I had a hard time making the figure recognizable as an elephant until I got the "tusks" right.

TIPS:

• This is easier for people with long fingers, because the longer the trunk (middle and third fingers), the more the figure resembles an elephant.
• To get maximum trunk length, rotate your hand slightly toward the light.
• Experiment with placement of the top of the head. Best position depends on the shape of your hands.

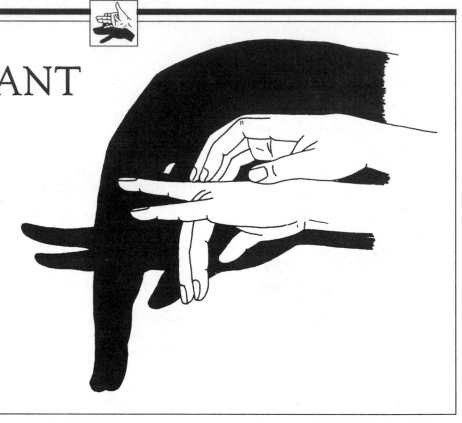

A GOAT

Notes

Another of Bursill's simpler creations. Of course, the horns are the key element (although the beard helps reinforce the notion that it's a goat instead of, say, a deer or a cow).

•Use this as the basis for creating a few horned creatures of your own.

TIPS:

• I always leave off the ear, because it forces me to twist my hands into a shape that looks more like the Blob than a goat.

• Don't worry about getting the mouth exactly right. It takes special coordination to keep the opening between the middle and third fingers small.

A RABBIT

Notes

You make a complete body, rather than just a head, with this one.

Instructions

1. Create a rabbit's head:
• Make a V with the first and middle fingers of your right hand.
• Fold your third finger and pinky in and cover them with your thumb as shown.

2. Hold the hand with its back toward you. Move it around in the light until it looks like a rabbit's head. Try moving the ears (first and middle fingers), cocking them slightly.

3. With your left hand, create the body:
• Bend the first and middle fingers over, as shown.
• Keep your third finger and pinky as straight as possible (but don't struggle with it).
• Extend your thumb as shown.

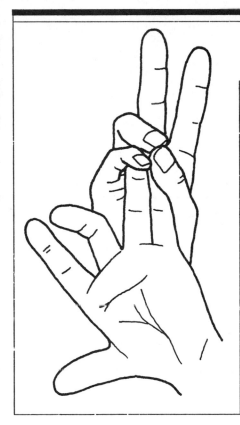

4. Now combine the 2 figures:
• Grasp the last 2 fingers of your left hand with the thumb and last 2 fingers of your right hand.
• Extend the first 2 fingers of the left hand to make the rabbit's paws.
• Extend the left thumb to create the rabbit's hind legs.

Advanced Shadow Rabbits:
• Move your pinky to give the illusion that the rabbit is munching.
• Practice lifting the rabbit's paws to its mouth.

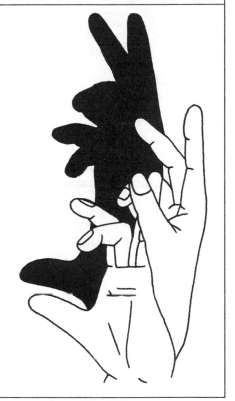

JUGGLING

Background

Juggling is just about as old as civilization. The ancient Egyptians, Greeks, and Romans practiced juggling. (They often mentioned it in books, manuscripts, and art.)

• Ancient coins that actually depict jugglers have been unearthed.

• The word *juggling* comes from the Latin *joculari*, which means "to jest."

• In medieval France, wandering minstrels were referred to as *jongleurs*, which evolved into the English version—juggler.

• Juggling looks a lot harder than it really is. It takes patience, but if you learn step by step, you'll be juggling in no time.

You'll Need:

Something to juggle
• At least 3 *identical*, small unbreakable objects. If you can hold 3 in 1 hand, then they're the right size for you.
• You can juggle anything you can toss and catch easily.

• Traditionally, small rubber balls are good juggling tools for beginners.
• Balls that are 2-1/4"–2-1/2" in diameter are the right size for most people. They should weigh about 4–6 ounces each.

• Or you may choose to start out with cloth-covered beanbags, which are available at toy stores and hobby shops.

• The key is comfort. Handling your juggling objects should feel good.

• Squash alert: Oranges, apples, and other fruit aren't recommended for beginners because they soften and split open when dropped repeatedly.

BEGINNERS' TIPS

Where to Practice

• Find a room or space where objects can't be broken by flying juggling objects. Outdoors is ideal. Overhead clearance is essential.

• Raise your arms straight overhead. You should have at least 2 more feet of clearance past your upraised fingertips.

Before You Start

• Relax. This is fun! Most people can pick up the basic moves in about 15 minutes. With daily practice, you can be really *good* at it.

• You learn juggling by taking things 1 step at a time. Repeat each move until you can perform it comfortably and confidently. Trying to go too quickly will only frustrate you.

Body Position

• Relax.

• Stand with your elbows close to your body and hands at about waist level, wrists loose.

• Hold the juggling objects (I'll call them balls for the purposes of these instructions) in the center of your hands, not with your fingers.

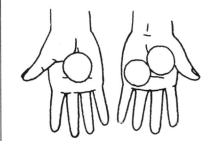

STEP 1: TOSSING 1 BALL

Notes

First, you must learn to toss 1 ball properly. This is the basic pattern for juggling anything; take it slowly and really absorb it.

Instructions

1. Hold 1 ball in your right hand.

2. Toss the ball up in a scooping motion so it arcs smoothly and lands in your left hand. Your left arm should not have to move far from the starting position described above.
• Your toss should arc at the height of the tips of your upraised hands.
• Ultimately, you should be able to

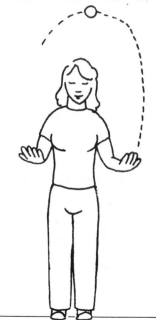

do this with your eyes closed and still catch the ball.

3. Now toss the ball back, from left hand to right.
• Developing a "point of consistent arc" is crucial—the balls should arc at about the same spot every time.

4. Practice this for a while—left hand to right, right hand to left, etc.

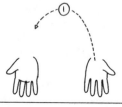

STEP 2: EXCHANGING BALLS

Notes

Next, you will learn to toss 2 balls properly. This will feel awkward at first. But keep practicing. In about 5 minutes you'll master the movements.

Instructions

1. Hold 1 ball in each hand.

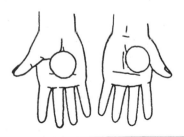

2. Toss 1 ball up in an arcing motion toward the other hand.
• When it reaches the top of its arc and starts to fall, you do 2 things simultaneously:
  a. Toss the second ball in a similar

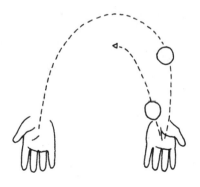

arc, in the opposite direction.
  b. Catch the first ball.

3. Now catch the *second* ball in the *first* hand.

Keep repeating this process until you feel comfortable with it.

Troubleshooting

Don't worry about mistakes—you'll probably make lots of them, like:
• throwing the first ball too high
• throwing the first ball too wide
• throwing both balls too far ahead of you so you end up lunging forward to catch them

STEP 3: JUGGLING 3 BALLS

Notes

• This is the big payoff. You already know the basic juggling moves by the time you've mastered step 2. Now you can add a third ball and actually juggle.

Instructions

1. Hold 2 balls in one hand and 1 ball in the other. We'll say there are 2 balls in your left hand and 1 in your right.

The balls in your left hand are balls #1 and #3. The ball in your right hand is #2.

2. Give ball #1 a good arcing toss toward your right hand.

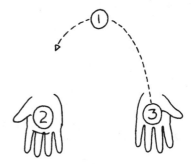

3. As ball #1 reaches the top of its arc and starts to drop, toss up ball #2 toward your left hand.

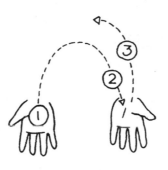

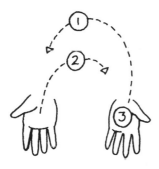

This should look very familiar. It's just like the action in step 2, which you just mastered.

4. As ball #1 comes down into your right hand, toss up ball #3 with your left hand. Just as you toss up ball #3, ball #2 should be dropping into your left hand.

Catch and release, catch and release—all in a scooping motion. Now you're juggling.

More Tips

• Remember: There's really only 1 object in the air at one time. The other 2 are in either hand.

• You can practice in front of a wall so the balls don't fly too far out in front of you. Then you won't have to run so far to retrieve them.

YO-YO TRICKS

Background

• Yo-yos originated in the prehistoric jungles of the Philippines, where they were used as weapons—a vine was tied around a grooved rock, and the rock was hurled at prey. If the hunter missed, he could retrieve the rock.

• The word *yo-yo* means "return" in Tagalog (a Philippine language).

• The yo-yo has been popular in Europe since ancient times. On a Greek vase dated around 500 B.C., there's a picture of a boy playing with a yo-yo.

• Yo-yos became popular in America in the late '20s when Donald Duncan marketed a yo-yo with a loop at the end of the string. This enabled yo-yos to "sleep" and yo-yoers to perform tricks with them.

You'll Need:

A Yo-yo

• Many types of yo-yos are available at toy stores, but the Duncan Imperial is the best for beginners and intermediates. It's cheap and reliable.

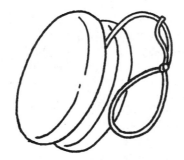

The proper string

• Most beginners just use the yo-yo as it comes, without adjusting the length of the string. But experts recommend that you cut the string to fit your body.

Here's how:

• Dangle the yo-yo so it's touching the ground between your feet.

• Then cut the string a few inches above your waist. That's the optimum length.

BEGINNERS' TIPS

The Loop

The standard yo-yo loop is a simple slipknot:

•Tie a small loop at the end of the string.
•Pull the longer length of string through it.

How to Hold the Yo-yo

•Slip the loop over your middle finger, a little above the knuckle.
•The knot should be on the inside of the finger.
•Cup your hand, palm up, and hold the yo-yo in your palm.

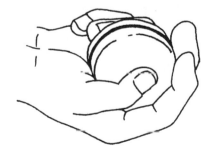

To Throw the Yo-yo

•Raise your arm and curl your wrist back, as if you were making a loose muscle.
•Bring your arm down and snap your wrist out, letting the yo-yo roll over the tips of your fingers.
•As the yo-yo reaches the end of the string, turn your palm over and give a little yank. If you time it right, the yo-yo will jump back up the string and into your hand.

THE SLEEPER

Notes

This is the essential yo-yo trick.
• Release the yo-yo and let it spin at the bottom of the string instead of pulling it back up immediately. Then you give it a yank, and it returns.
• Experts say the harder tricks need 6 to 8 seconds of "sleeping" time, from throw to recovery.

TIPS:

• Start by making the yo-yo sleep for just a few seconds. Increase the time gradually.
• If a yo-yo won't sleep, the string may be wound too tight. Unwind it, let it fall, and untwist about 10 times.
• The faster you make the yo-yo spin, the longer it will sleep.

Instructions

1. Throw the yo-yo, snapping your wrist with as much force as is comfortable.
• The more force you put into the spin, the longer it can sleep.

2. As the yo-yo gets to the bottom, don't tug it back up—"cushion" it by letting your wrist go a little limp. It will hang at the end of the string, spinning.
• Variation: try swinging it as it sleeps.

3. Before the yo-yo stops spinning, give a little tug, and it will return.

WALKING THE DOG

Notes

This is the classic trick to work on after you're able to make your yo-yo sleep. Lower the spinning yo-yo to the floor, and it will "walk" for a short distance on its own.

TIPS:

• Most people have a hard time getting more than a few bounces out of a "walking" yo-yo. One reason: beginners tend to let the string loosen when they set the yo-yo down. The string must be tight for this trick to work.
• When you can "walk the dog" on a normal surface, try letting your yo-yo "walk" on newspaper. It makes a buzzing noise.

Instructions

1. Throw a sleeper.

2. Swing the yo-yo a little in front of you and gently lower it to the floor.
• Keep a soft touch.

3. "Walk" the spinning yo-yo in front of you, as you would with a dog on a leash.

4. Before it stops spinning, give the yo-yo a slight yank with the "leash," and it will return to your hand.

AROUND THE CORNER

Notes

This is a sort of weird trick that requires body control as well as yo-yo control. It's a standard yo-yo tournament trick.

• You'll drape the sleeping yo-yo over your shoulder, then swing it forward over your body for the return.

TIPS:

• If your string gets messed up, you can change it. Packets of yo-yo strings are available at game stores.

• Wax for the strings is also available. Waxing the top 6" of the string makes the yo-yo perform better.

• If you do change it, be careful not to scrape the axle—a damaged axle will render the yo-yo useless.

Instructions

1. Throw a fast sleeper.

2. Carefully move the yo-yo around your body, in back of your shoulder.

3. Flick your wrist forward, and the yo-yo will hop over your shoulder.

4. As it moves up and around, keep it straight and level. When it reaches the end of the string, it will return to your hand.

SKIN THE CAT

Notes

This also requires some body control, but it's relatively easy once you get a feel for it. Feels good, too.

• You'll pull the yo-yo string over your free hand and flip the yo-yo into the air, making it circle and return.

Instructions

1. Throw a fast sleeper.

2. Slide the middle finger of your free hand down the yo-yo string, a few inches from the loop.

3. With your yo-yo hand, pull the string back over either your first or middle finger (whatever's best for you), until the finger is about 6" from the yo-yo.

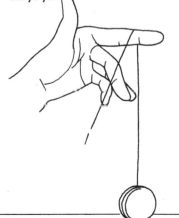

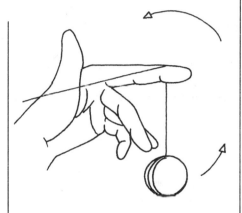

4. With your first or middle finger, gently flip the yo-yo out and up. The yo-yo will circle all the way around your free hand and then return to your yo-yo hand.

ROCK THE BABY

Notes

If you're like me, you've been trying to get this trick right since you first learned to yo-yo. It's tough.

• The idea is to keep the yo-yo spinning while you swing it inside a triangle made with the yo-yo string, then let it go and have it return to you.

• It's also called "Rock the Cradle."

TIPS:

• Practice making the cradle (the triangle) with a yo-yo that's not spinning. You've got to get the motion and position down pat.

• Experts say that you need at least a 6-second sleep to perform this trick.

Instructions

1. Throw a fast sleeper.

2. Reach down to about the middle of the string with your free hand and drape the string toward you, over your fingers.

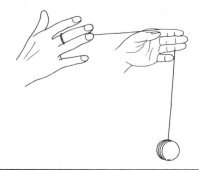

3. Raise the string with your free hand, fingers spread.

• As you lift the string, reach down and grab it 4-6" above the yo-yo with your yo-yo hand.

• You should now have an upside-down triangle. The yo-yo is still spinning.

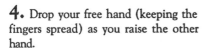

4. Drop your free hand (keeping the fingers spread) as you raise the other hand.

• You're now holding a triangle.

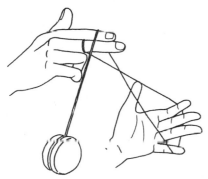

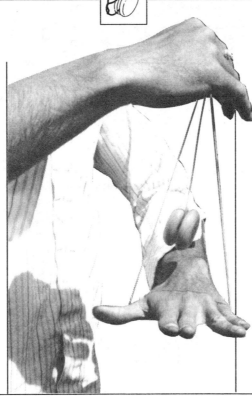

5. While the yo-yo sleeps, gently swing it back and forth through the triangle.

6. The proper return: Gently swing the yo-yo out in front of you. Let it drop as you let go of the cradle.

Note: The palm of your hand can face either up or down, depending on what's easier for you. I've always kept my palm down, but I've seen people do it the opposite way, too.

SHOOTING MARBLES

Background

People have been shooting marbles since prehistoric times. Archaeologists have found "small balls of clay, flint, and stone" in European caves.
• The Aztecs and ancient Egyptians played marbles. So did the Romans; Emperor Augustus obsessively played a "marble" game using polished nuts.
• The British brought marbles to America (George Washington and Thomas Jefferson shot them as kids), but the first marbles weren't manufactured in the U.S. until 1884. They were made of clay. Glass came later.
• Shooting marbles isn't as popular as it once was, but marbles are still readily available at toy stores.

You'll Need:

A large marble

• Called a "shooter," a "taw," or a "bowler." You flick it at other marbles, trying to hit them.
• According to the official rules, the shooter marble must be "at least 1/2" and not more than 3/4" in diameter."

Regular-Size Marbles

• Called "mibs" or "ducks."
• According to the official rules, they "must be round, made of glass [although you can also get steel and clay ones], and of uniform size, measuring not more than 5/8" in diameter."

Different Types of Marbles

To some players, the aesthetics of marbles are as important as the game itself. Among the types of marbles available (you can guess what they look like from the names):
• Cat's-Eyes
• Black Beauties
• Swirled Glass
• Blood Rubies

BEGINNERS' TRICKS

Learn to Shoot a Marble

If you've never played marbles, the first trick is just to learn to shoot one. Later, the challenge will be to do it accurately.

• According to the pros, the most important part of shooting a marble is developing backspin, so when the shooter hits a mib, the shooter will stop rolling—leaving you in a good position to fire at other mibs.

• Doing this right takes a *lot* of practice. It took me a month just to learn to flick it right…and another month to get even a little backspin.

Here's How You Shoot:

• Hold the shooter between the first

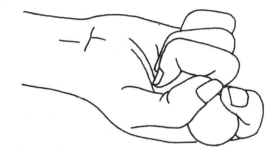

and middle fingers.

• Cock your thumb so the nail is pressing up against the shooter. (The shooter is held in place by squeezing it with your first finger.)

• Now put your hand down, with at least 1 knuckle touching the ground. This is called "knuckling down." It's an essential part of shooting marbles.

(Important rule: One knuckle *must* be touching the ground at all times.)

• Flick your thumbnail against the shooter, but don't move your hand—that's called "hunching," and it's against the rules. You forfeit a turn if you "hunch."

• You don't have to flick your shooter hard—just smoothly and accurately.

LAGGING

Notes

This is the traditional way to figure out who goes first in any marbles game. It's sort of a trick by itself, like pitching pennies.

• The idea is to toss or shoot a marble at a line about 15 feet away and get it as close to the line as possible.

Instructions

1. Draw 2 lines about 1-1/2 feet apart.

2. Draw another line about 15 feet away. This is called the "pitch" line.

3. Stand behind the pitch line, facing the other 2 lines you drew. The line closest to you is the "lag" line. The back line is the out-of-bounds line.

4. Either knuckle down behind the pitch line and shoot your marble at the lag line or stand and toss your shooter at it.

• The goal is to get your shooter as close to the lag line as possible—in front or in back of it—without crossing the out-of-bounds line.

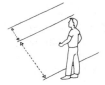

OUT OF BOUNDS

THE WINNER

5. Whoever gets his shooter closest to the lag line (in bounds) goes first.

THE CLASSIC MARBLE GAME

Notes

This game, called "Ringer," is played by 2 people at a time. You make a ring in the dirt with a stick (or, if you want a flatter surface, on the sidewalk with chalk—or even on the floor with string) and lay out 13 marbles in a cross pattern. Then you take turns shooting at the marbles, trying to knock them out of the ring.
•The person who knocks the most marbles out of the ring is the winner. Or, if you're playing cutthroat, you get to keep the marbles you knock out.

Remember:
•At least 1 knuckle must be touching the ground when you shoot.
•You *can't* move your hand.

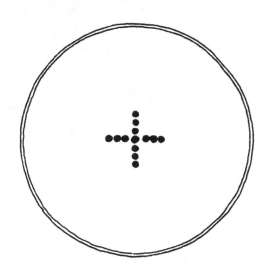

According to the official rules, your circle should be 10 feet in diameter. But if you're just learning, try making it somewhere between 3 and 6 feet.

Instructions

1. Make a 10-foot circle with a stick, chalk, or string (depending on the playing surface).

2. Lay 13 marbles in the center, as shown in preceding diagram.

3. Each player kneels outside the circle and "knuckles down."

4. Take turns. Flick your shooter into the circle, trying to hit 1 of the marbles and knock it outside the ring.
• Rule: you can use *only* your thumb to do the flicking.

5. If you miss, or if the shooter rolls out of the ring, pick up your shooter and wait for your next turn. On the next turn, you can start anywhere around the circle.

6. If you knock a marble out of the ring and the shooter stays inside the ring, leave the shooter where it is and go again. Keep going until you miss.
• Each marble you knock out of the ring is a point. Whoever knocks out 7 marbles wins.

PAPER AIRPLANES

Background

• Paper airplane enthusiasts speculate that Leonardo da Vinci was the first to experiment with paper flight. Actually, his planes were constructed out of parchment.

• Paper flight history: The Montgolfier brothers came up with the concept of the hot air balloon in 1783 when they happened to hang a paper bag over a wood fire.

• Paper airplanes were recognized as a modern art form when *Scientific American* magazine sponsored "The First International Paper Airplane Competition" in December 1966. They received an astonishing number of complex entries, which spawned a series of contests and books.

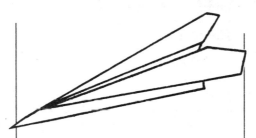

You'll Need:

Paper

The more intricate paper airplane designs—and there are some astounding ones—utilize everything from glue to drafting equipment. But the planes included here are simple. For 3, all you need is a piece of 8-1/2" x 11" paper. The fourth requires scissors, with which you'll make a single cut.

Optional:

• Paper clips, which some planemakers use to weight down the tips of their planes.

• A stapler. Staples can add both weight and stability to the plane. Of course, they can also make the plane too heavy—it's your call.

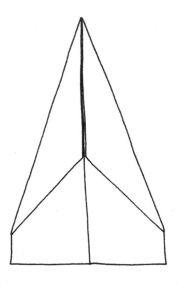

BASIC PAPER PLANE

Notes

This is the plane everyone in elementary school could make—even me. If you've never made a paper airplane, you should start with this one.

• All you need is a regular piece of 8 1/2" x 11" paper (notebook size, you recall).

TIPS:

• Don't use newspaper.
• Work on a clean surface.
• Try to get the folds right the first time. If you keep going back and re-creasing the paper, the plane will lose its form.
• On the other hand, if you don't get the folds exactly right, who cares?

Instructions

1. Fold the paper in half lengthwise to make a crease. Then unfold it.

2. Fold the corners at 1 end into the middle to meet the crease.

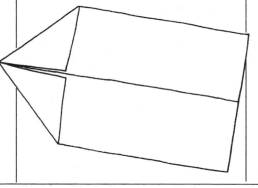

3. Fold the corners into the middle again so it looks like the illustration.

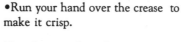

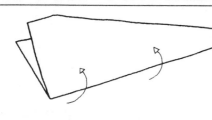

4. Fold it over at the center crease. Run your hand over the crease to make it crisp.

5. Fold the wings over as shown above.
Tip: It's easier to fold and crease the wings from front to back.

•Run your hand over the crease to make it crisp.

To throw the plane:

•Grasp the plane about midway down the fuselage between your thumb and first finger.
•Experiment to see how it can fly: first, toss it gently, with a slight upward motion; then rear back and throw it like a missile.

Variation: Try folding the ends of the wings down to make flaps. They seem to hold the plane aloft longer.

BASIC PLANE #2

Notes

I've had a lot of fun with this out-doors. If the wind catches it right, it seems to go forever.

• All you need is an 8-1/2" x 11" sheet of paper, but I think adding a paper clip to the nose of this plane gives it just the right amount of weight for a long flight.

Instructions

1. Fold the paper in half lengthwise.
• Leave it folded.

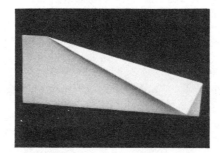

2. Fold the corners at 1 end down at an angle, even with the lengthwise crease.
• Make the fold good and crisp.

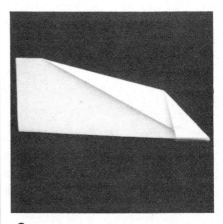

3. Fold the corners at the same end again.
• Again, they should be even with the lengthwise crease.

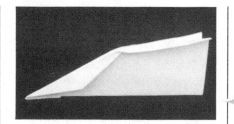

4. Fold the top corner down again, as shown. This fold is a little tough because there are now several folds on top of each other

5. Fold the top edges down about 1/2", angled slightly up. These are going to be the wing flaps.

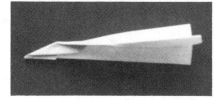

6. Fold the wings down., angling them slightly up.
•Wings are about 2-1/2" wide.

8. Optional: Attach a paper clip to the front end of the plane.
To throw: toss it straight ahead.

GLIDER

Notes

A friend of mine swears this is the easiest paper airplane to make, and it *is* easy—but it still flies incredibly well. It doesn't seem to work outdoors, though.

• All you need is an 8-1/2" x 11" sheet of paper.

Instructions

1. Fold the shorter edge of the paper over, creasing it about 1/3 of the way down (3-3/4").

2. Fold the paper in half lengthwise, just to get a good crease. Then unfold it.

3. Fold the corners in so they meet at the lengthwise crease, about 1-1/2" from the edge.

4. Fold the edge over about 1-3/4", as shown.

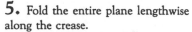

5. Fold the entire plane lengthwise along the crease.
•The paper folds should be on the outside.

6. Fold the wings down, angled slightly. The tail edge should be about 2-1/4", the front edge about 1-1/2".

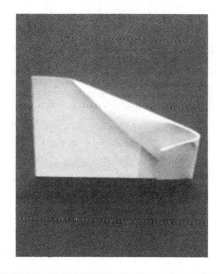

To Throw the Plane

Toss it straight ahead, holding it toward the front, between your thumb and first fingers.
•It doesn't require a lot of force. Toss gently, and it will take off.
•If it unfolds, try attaching a small piece of tape at the top to keep the wings closed.

SUPERSONIC

Notes

I love this plane. I learned it from the book *More Best Paper Aircraft*, by Campbell Morris, which I highly recommend to paper plane dabblers.
- Again, use an 8-1/2" x 11" sheet of paper.
- This plane requires a single scissors cut.
- Morris suggests using tape, but I've never bothered.

Instructions

1. Fold the paper in half lengthwise.

2. Fold the upper corners down at an angle (about 1-1/2") as shown.

3. Fold the top corners down at an angle again (about 2-1/2") to meet the original lengthwise crease.

4. Now, using scissors, cut off the back corner on a diagonal line, as shown.
•Your folded paper should now be a triangle.

5. Fold down the top of the triangle on each side. These are the wings.
• **The wing** crease should be about 3/4" from the bottom (fuselage).

6. Fold the wing back up on a new fold, about 1/2" down from the original one.

7. Fold down the wing flaps as shown.

8. Crease the wings so they're drooping slightly.

Fly the plane.

TRICKS WITH TOPS

Background

People have been playing with tops for thousands of years. The first tops were probably made from shells, acorns, or other natural material.
• In ancient Rome, the famous statesman Cato recommended tops for children. "Better than dice," he advised.
• In the early years of Christianity, tops were part of a church ritual.
• The most popular variety of top in the U.S., the "peg" top, originated in ancient Japan.
• By the 1300s it was common in England, and by the late 1700s it was a fixture in Colonial America.
• Today tops are almost a novelty, often hard to find—even in toy stores.

You'll Need:

A peg top
• Wooden and plastic tops are available...but not everywhere. Keep looking. The only one I could find locally was an "old-fashioned" wooden top made by a company called Shackman. It's hardly a precision instrument, but it works.

A string
• Should be about 5 feet long.
• Make sure it's the right thickness—a lightweight string can keep the top from spinning.

BEGINNERS' TIPS

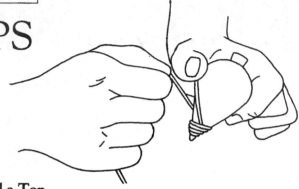

Prepare the String

Tie a knot in one end of the string. (The one that will be wrapped around the top.)

At the other end, give yourself something to hold on to. You can:

• tie a loop for your finger
• thread the string through a button and tie a knot to keep it on
• wrap the string around your finger

Some tops come with a metal ring attached to the string—that's fine, too.

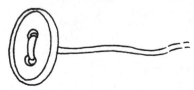

How to Wind a Top

1. Hold the knotted end of the string against the top with your thumb, as shown.

2. Wrap the other end of the string around the top, starting at the bottom and working your way up.
• Wrap counterclockwise if you're right-handed, clockwise if you're left-handed.

3. When you've wound the string around the top, put the loop or ring around the middle finger of your throwing hand.
• If you're using a button, put it behind your middle and third fingers, with the string between those fingers.

HOW TO THROW A TOP

Notes

Spinning a top only seems easy *after* you've figured it out. Although this is the easiest way to spin a top, it will definitely take a while to get the feel of it.

• After you get it, move on to the rest of the tricks in this section.

TIPS:

• These instructions are written for right-handers. Just reverse them if you're a lefty.

• If the launch doesn't work, it's probably because you're pulling incorrectly—either too hard and fast...or the opposite, too slow and soft. Find that middle ground, and the top will spin.

Instructions

1. Wind the top. Put the loop around the middle finger, or the button between your middle and third fingers.

• Hold the top between your thumb and fingertips.

• Kneel with your hand stretched out in front of you, about a foot off the floor. The tip of the top should be pointing straight down.

2. Flick your wrist and forearm away from your body. As you complete the flick, pull your hand back toward you and end it with another slight flick. **Note:** Keep your arm parallel to the floor.

• The *second* flick is what launches the top.

THE OVERHAND THROW

Notes

This is a lot harder than the normal throw, but you get more speed when you throw a top overhand—so you can do more tricks with it. After a while you'll be able to pinpoint the spot where you want the top to land.

TIPS:

• Since the top is coming from a different direction this time, you wind it in the opposite direction from the first method. If you're right-handed, you now wind your top clockwise. If you're left-handed, you wind it counterclockwise.

• Make sure your string is long enough (5 feet) and heavy enough.

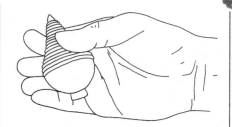

Instructions

1. Grasp the top between thumb and fingertips, holding it upside down, as shown. The tip is pointing skyward.

2. Hold your arm out to the side, slightly higher than your head. Reach back to throw.

• Keep your arm pretty straight;

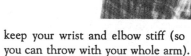

keep your wrist and elbow stiff (so you can throw with your whole arm).

3. Bring your arm around and release the top, aiming it at a point about a yard in front of you on the ground.

• It should flip over by itself and spin. But if it doesn't, keep trying. You'll get it eventually.

THE JUMPING TOP

Notes

After conquering the overhead spin, you can experiment with ways to make your top perform for you.
• In this trick you spin the top, then wrap the string around the tip while it's still spinning. The top will leap into the air like a rocket, and you'll catch it in your open hand.

Instructions

1. Launch the top with an overhand throw.

2. Take 1 end of the string in each hand and make a counterclockwise loop on the ground, around the top.

3. Tighten the loop and carefully lift it, catching the top close to the point.

4. The top will leap into the air. Stick your hand out and catch it on your palm. If you do it correctly, the top will keep spinning on your hand. **Note:** Be gentle with the top. If you hoist the string too forcefully, the top will jump too far for you to catch it.

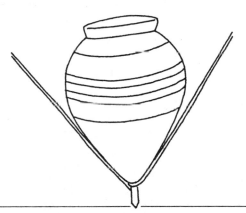

THE RETURN TOP

Notes

This trick requires string control and a lot of patience.

• The idea: If you pull the string back as you throw the top, you can make the top jump back to you before it ever touches the ground.

TIPS:

• As you practice, concentrate on getting the right pull.

• If you pull too hard, the top will zoom back, out of control.

• If you pull too softly, you'll just have a normal overhand throw.

• The best pull is one that brings the top back to your hand without making you bend over or reach for it.

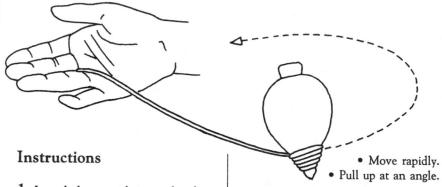

• Move rapidly.
• Pull up at an angle.

Instructions

1. Launch the top with an overhand throw.

2. Before the top completely unwinds from the string, yank back on the string.

3. If you do it correctly (remember that it takes a lot of practice), the top will return to you in the air.

4. Catch it in your open hand.

THE HANDOFF

Notes

After you've mastered the 2 previous tricks and can reliably catch the spinning top in your hand, you can embellish them with these moves.

Instructions

1. Launch the top with an overhand throw.

2. Do 1 of the previous 2 tricks; catch the spinning top in your hand.

3. Put your hands together. Surprisingly, you can transfer the top from 1 hand to the other.
• Try moving your top from fingertip

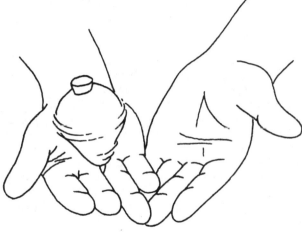

to fingertip.

4. More advanced moves:
• Raise 1 leg and "walk" the top

from 1 hand to the other under it.
• Hold your hands behind your back and "walk" the top from hand to hand without being able to see it.

BALLOON TRICKS

Background

• The original balloons were animal bladders. Galileo, for example, used a pig's bladder when experimenting with methods to determine the weight of air.

• English scientist Michael Faraday is believed to have made the first rubber balloon in 1824. A year later, do-it-yourself balloon kits were sold to the British public.

• Toward the end of the 19th century, balloons were generally available in Europe. But they weren't manufactured in America until 1907.

• It wasn't until 1931 that the first modern latex balloon was created. That made it possible to produce balloons cheaply as toys and decorations.

You'll Need:

Round latex balloons
• Except when you're making water balloons, it's best to use 11" balloons that are made for use with helium—they're thicker and last longer than the typical "party" balloons.

• Buy them at stores that specialize in balloons (look up *Balloons* in the yellow pages—you'll be surprised at how many stores there are) or at gift and party stores.

• For several of the tricks, you specifically need *clear* latex balloons (they have no pigment, so you can see through them). These are also available at balloon and party stores.

• Water balloons are made to be broken, so use cheap balloons.

You Also Need:

• Cellophane tape
• A pin
• A plastic drinking straw
• A length of kite string or nylon fishing line (at least 8-12 feet)
• A penny
• A towel

BEGINNERS' TIPS

Inflating Round Balloons

• Stretch a balloon before blowing it up. It's easier to inflate.

• The higher quality the balloon, the harder it is to inflate, because better balloons are made of thicker latex. The consolation: they last longer.

• When it's cold, balloons are harder to inflate. But when it's hot out, the opposite is true—you can easily over-blow a balloon and pop it.

• Some balloons have wide necks, some have narrow necks. Wide necks inflate more easily.

How Much Air?

• You can tell when a balloon is inflated to full capacity because it gets sort of transparent (you can see right through the color), and you can feel the tightness of the rubber.

• It's better to underinflate a balloon than to fill it up. The less a balloon is inflated, the thicker the wall is—so the more abuse it can take.

Sealing a Balloon

• Most people know the basics about tying off a balloon once it's inflated. But there's a trick to it:

• After inflating the balloon, hold the neck in 1 hand, pinching it shut between thumb and first finger.

• Then, with your free hand, stretch the neck up and twist it a few times.

• Then tie it off.

• The twisting is what keeps the air from escaping after it's tied.

These activities are a few of the projects in *Superloon's Amazing Balloon Book*, by Dr. Inflate-O. If you are interested in purchasing a copy, write to Balloons, #25, 1400 Shattuck Ave., Berkeley, CA 94709.

THE UNPOPPABLE BALLOON

Notes

This is one of the simplest balloon tricks there is. But if you can find some people who've never seen it before, you'll impress them.

You'll Need:
- A piece of cellophane tape (or any brand of cellophane tape)
- A balloon
- A pin

Instructions

1. Inflate the balloon. Put a piece of tape on it. Make sure the tape is on securely.

2. Slowly stick a pin into the center of the tape. Amazingly, the balloon will not burst.

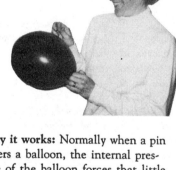

Why it works: Normally when a pin enters a balloon, the internal pressure of the balloon forces that little hole open and tears the balloon apart. But tape holds the balloon together, so the pinhole remains a tiny hole; air will slowly leak out, but the balloon won't pop.

A PENNY IN A BALLOON

Notes

Most people don't realize they can put things inside balloons—marbles, little plastic cars, a Tootsie Roll, anything that rolls around or makes noise. My favorite is a penny, which will roll around the inside of a balloon on its side when the balloon is rotated.

• Use a clear latex balloon, so you can watch the penny spin.

TIPS: Use an 11" balloon and under-inflate it. As the penny circles the balloon, it will wear a groove in the wall and eventually the balloon will pop in your hand—if you underinflate, the balloon will last longer.

Instructions

1. Put the penny inside the uninflated balloon. If balloon neck is too thin, insert your fingers on either side of the neck. Stretch it out and drop the penny in.

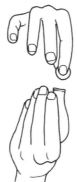

2. Inflate the balloon. Either seal it or hold the neck tightly so no air escapes.

Caution: blow down, so the penny doesn't roll back into your throat.

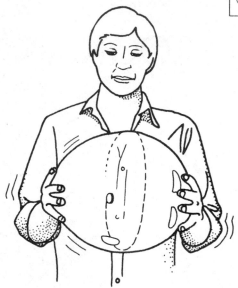

3. Holding the balloon in 2 hands, rotate it. (Bring your hands toward you, then up and around.) At first the penny will bounce around inside the balloon. But keep going—eventually it will flip onto its side and begin rolling around the interior surface. Once it gets going, the penny will zoom around on its own.

And try these in a balloon...

A ping-pong ball. Zooms around the inside of the balloon.

A Tootsie Roll. Makes a great thumping noise.

BALLOON-IN-A-BALLOON

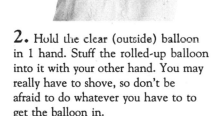

Notes

You've probably seen balloons inside of balloons before and wondered how it's done. It looks intriguing, but it's actually pretty simple.

You'll need:
• A clear or translucent 11" latex balloon
• A solid-color latex balloon that's the same size as or a little smaller than the clear one (It's easier with a smaller balloon.)

TIPS:
• The clear or translucent balloon goes on the outside.
• This takes a lot of lung power.

Instructions

1. Hold the uninflated solid-color balloon (the inside one) in 2 hands.
• Stretch it out to make it easier to inflate.
• Twist it as tightly as you can (as if you're wringing out a cloth).
• Make it into a small cigar shape.

2. Hold the clear (outside) balloon in 1 hand. Stuff the rolled-up balloon into it with your other hand. You may really have to shove, so don't be afraid to do whatever you have to to get the balloon in.
• When you've got 1 balloon inside the other, hold the 2 necks together.

Note: Beware of fingernails.

3. After 1 balloon is inside the other, shake both around so the inside balloon straightens out. The neck should be unrolled.

4. You now have 1 balloon neck sticking out from the other. The inside balloon neck should be slightly higher than the outside balloon neck.

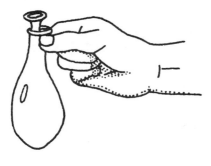

5. Pinch the inside balloon's neck to the side.

6. Blow into the outside balloon *only*, still holding the neck of the inside balloon to 1 side. This takes a heap o' blowin'.

7. Partially inflate the outside balloon. Be sure to underinflate it.

8. Pinch the neck of the outside balloon and inflate the inside balloon. This takes more lung power (try it in short bursts). As you blow up the inside balloon, you're also blowing up the outside balloon—so both will get bigger. (That's why you underinflated the outside balloon.)

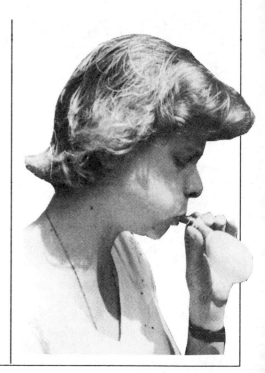

9. Stretch out the neck of the inside balloon and tie a knot in it. This is probably the hardest part of the trick. Then, with one finger, shove the balloon all the way into the outside balloon.

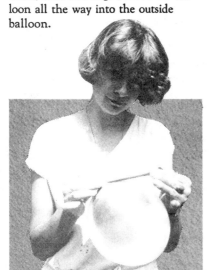

10. Tie a knot in the neck of outside balloon. Shake it, and the inside balloon will come free and bounce around inside.

BALLOON MONORAIL

Notes

Using string and straws, you can build a balloon-powered vehicle that zooms across the room on its own.

You'll Need:
• A balloon (the bigger the better—bigger balloons travel farther)
• Cellophane tape
• A plastic drinking straw
• Kite string or fish-line, and scissors
• A paper clip

TIP:
You can do this inside or outside, anywhere where you can tie each end of a piece of string to something—2 trees, a doorknob and chair, etc.

Instructions

1. Cut a 10-15-foot length of string. Thread the string through the straw.

2. Tie each end of the string to something so the string is stretched out, taut, between the two points.

3. Inflate the balloon, twist the neck, and use the paper clip to seal it temporarily.

4. Tape the inflated balloon to the straw.
• Hold it as close to the straw as possible.
• Wrap 2 pieces of tape over the straw and around the balloon—1 in the front, 1 in the back.

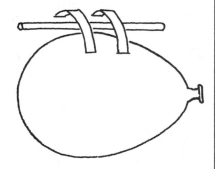

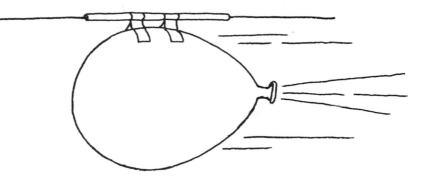

5. Move the balloon to the launching point.

• If the string is fairly level, it doesn't matter where you start.

• If the string is slanted up in 1 direction, take the balloon to the highest point and start it there—the monorail runs fastest when it's going downhill.

6. Ready for blast-off: hold the neck as you remove the paper clip.

7. Release the balloon. It will zoom across the room to the end of the string.

8. Surprisingly, the monorail balloon is reusable in most cases—so start all over again.

Set up 2 monorails side by side and race them.

WATER BALLOONS

Notes

It's hard to believe, but there may be some underprivileged adults who've never had the pleasure of dropping a water balloon from a building onto the sidewalk (and maybe a pedestrian) below. Or tossing one to a friend and yelling "Catch!" as it splatters all over him or her. To rectify that, here are instructions for making water balloons.

TIPS:
Use a bunch of **cheap balloons. No** sense wasting good balloons or— worse—tossing a water balloon and watching it bounce instead of burst.

Instructions

1. Stretch the neck of a balloon over the nozzle of a faucet.

2. Turn on the cold water slowly; let it fill the balloon. Hold 1 hand underneath the balloon for support and 1 hand on the neck.

3. Turn the water off when the balloon starts to feel heavy. Keep supporting it underneath.

4. With your free hand, remove the balloon from the faucet. Pinch the neck to keep the water in and seal it by tying a knot in the neck.

WATER BALLOON SLINGSHOT

Notes

There are 2 ways to get a water balloon slingshot—make one or buy one.

• The store-bought slingshots are fantastic. They can propel water balloons as far as a city block— definitely a new dimension in delinquency. Check out your local balloon store to find one.

• The alternative is comparatively tame, but it's the best homemade water balloon launcher I've ever played with.

• All you need is a towel and some balloons.

Instructions

1. Put a water balloon in the center of a large towel.

2. Grab both ends of the towel and swing it over your head as fast as you can.

3. Let 1 of the ends of the towel go as you swing it. Hold on to the other end. **The balloon will soar away.**

It takes time, but eventually you'll be able to pick out and hit a target.

A BALLOON ANIMAL

Background

Surprisingly, this is a fairly new field. Although entertainers have been making animals out of *round* balloons for many years, it wasn't until the late '60s that they began twisting single thin balloons (also called "pencil" balloons) into animals.

• The key to the craze was a book called *One Balloon Zoo*, published in the '60s. Balloon sculpture became popular almost overnight and, during the '70s, became a standard part of clown and magic acts.

• This is easier than it looks; the real trick is blowing up the thin balloons, which require an incredible amount of air pressure. Luckily, you can solve that problem with a pump.

You'll Need:

Pencil Balloons
• Several types are available, but the one generally recommended by professionals is called the #260. Most balloon stores carry them.
• They're cheapest by the gross (144), and you'll easily use that many once you get going.

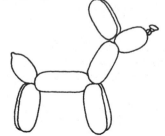

A Pump
• Most people shouldn't bother trying to inflate pencil balloons on their own—it takes too much energy and lung power.
• Just pick up a pump. You can get a decent one for under $5, or pick up Aaron Hsu-Flanders' *Balloon Animals*, the best selling kit put out by Contemporary Books. It includes an instruction manual, balloons, and a specially designed pump. It's a good, easy way to get started with balloon sculpture.

INFLATING THE BALLOON

Notes

I'm assuming you're using a pump. If for some reason you insist on using your lungs, instructions can be found in a book entitled *Basic Balloon Sculpture*, by George Schindler. Good luck.

TIPS:

• Stretch the balloon before inflating; it softens the rubber and adds a few inches to the length of the balloon.
• Don't inflate the balloon completely. Leave a part of the balloon uninflated so air can move around inside as you twist the balloon.
• The uninflated part of the balloon is called a "tail." The rule of thumb: leave 1/2" of the balloon uninflated for each twist you have to make in a balloon animal.

Instructions

1. Slip the end of the balloon over the tip of the pump.

2. Hold the balloon on as you pump air into it. Leave at least a 2-1/2" tail. Most beginnners overinflate, so start by purposely underinflating the balloon.

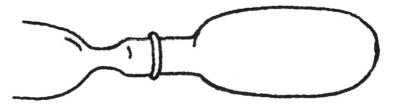

TYING THE BALLOON

Notes

If you're inexperienced at it, this can be frustrating at first. But you'll get used to it.

TIPS:
• There is no "right way" to seal a balloon. Any way that works for you is perfectly acceptable.
• Before tying the balloon, let a little air out of it so the neck is lengthened —then stretch the neck out 4"–5". This gives you something to grasp as you tie the knot
• As you tie, hold on to the balloon firmly. Otherwise, it may fly out of your hand.

Instructions

1. Hold the balloon neck between your thumb and first finger.

2. Stretch out the neck and wrap it around your first and second fingers.

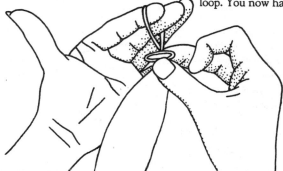

3. Separate your first and second fingers, making a space between them. Slip the neck of the balloon into this space, as shown.

4. Holding the neck, remove your first and second fingers from the loop. You now have a knot; tighten it.

THE BASIC DOG

Notes

This is taken from *Balloon Animals*, published by Contemporary Books.
• The dog is about the simplest animal you can make, but it's still a thrill. The first time I did it, I was so amazed that I could bend and twist a balloon without breaking it that it didn't matter *what* I made. Then I started looking at my creation and discovered that it's important to get the proportions right. When I made the ears too big, for example, the rest of the body looked absurd.

TIPS:

The Basic Dog teaches you many of the twisting techniques you need to know for other animals.

Instructions

1. Inflate the balloon, leaving a 3–5" tail.

2. With your thumb and first finger, pinch the balloon 3" from the knot and twist it 3 or 4 full turns. You now have a 3" bubble at the top of the balloon.
• Hold on to it gently to keep it from untwisting.
• This is the dog's nose.

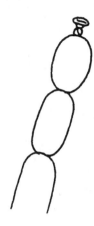

3. Make a second bubble.
• With thumb and first finger, pinch the balloon 3" from the first bubble.
• Now twist your hands in opposite directions, turning the balloon 3 or 4 full turns.
• You now have 2 bubbles. (The second one is part of the dog's ears.)
• Don't let them untwist.

4. Fold the 2 bubbles over so they're alongside the rest of the balloon.

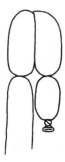

5. Pinch the balloon 3" down from the fold (even with the first twist) to make a third bubble.

• Don't let the other 2 bubbles untwist.

• This is the other half of the dog's ears.

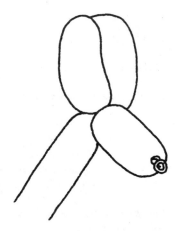

6. To finish the ears: Twist the second and third bubbles together, 2–3 full turns.

• The ears and nose should be locked together now, so you can stop holding them.

7. Now make another bubble, pinching the balloon 3" down from the ears and nose.

• Twist the balloon 2-3 full turns and hold it gently to prevent it from untwisting.

• This is the neck.

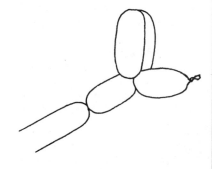

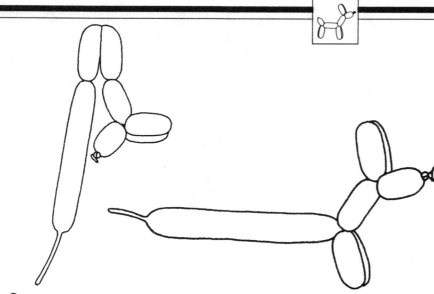

8. Make the front legs exactly the same way you made the ears.

• Make another 3" bubble, twisting the balloon several times.

• Fold it over, alongside the rest of the balloon.

• Pinch the balloon 3" down from the fold, making another bubble.

• Twist the 2 leg bubbles together, 2-3 full turns.

• This should lock the legs and neck in place, so you don't have to keep holding them.

9. Now make another bubble, pinching the balloon 3" down from the legs.

• Twist the balloon 2-3 full turns and hold it gently to prevent it from untwisting.

• This is the body.

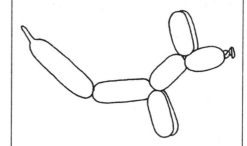

129

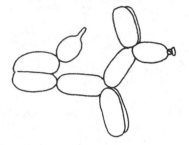

10. Make the back legs exactly the way you made the front ones.
- Make another 3" bubble, twisting the balloon several times.
- Fold it over, alongside the rest of the balloon.
- Pinch the balloon 3" down from the fold, making another bubble.
- Twist the leg bubbles together, 2-3 full turns.
- This should lock the legs and body in place so you don't have to keep holding them.
- Make sure you've left a little bubble at the end—that's the dog's tail.

11. Now you've got it. Don't be surprised if the dog looks a little weird—getting the proportions right comes with experience. Keep making dogs, and you'll work it out.

130

CAT'S CRADLE

Background

• Cat's Cradle is the oldest 2-person game in the history of mankind.

• Since prehistoric times, string games have been played by people all over the world—including North American Indians, the Incas, western Europeans, central Africans, and the Japanese. Eskimos believed that figures made from string possessed supernatural powers.

• Long before string was available, people used strands of braided human hair as well as animal sinews, tendons, and intestines for games and rites.

• In America, for some reason, this is a game played primarily by girls. So for most men, it's a new experience.

A few of the dozens of Cat's Cradle moves—enough to get you started or refresh your memory—are included in the following pages.

Note: To save space, I've referred to the partners as "he" in these instructions. Nothing political intended. Actually, the models' names are Penelope and Mel.

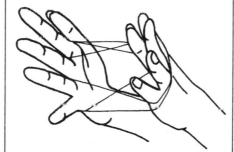

You'll Need:

Nylon or cotton string

• A length of string about 6 feet. Thicker string is easier to work with.

Note: The string must be as easy to *untangle* as it is to play with.

• Don't use thin twine or packing string; it will cut your fingers.

Make a Loop

To start: Tie your length of string into a loop. Cut off the excess.

THE OPENING POSITION

Notes

The first position is the Cradle.

Instructions

1. Face your partner.
• Put your hands through the loop of string, palms facing each other. Keep your thumb outside the loop.
• Spread your hands until the string is taut.

2. Loop the string around each hand once.

3. Slide your right middle finger under the loop circling your left hand.
• Pull back and make the string taut.
• Now slide your left middle finger under the loop around your right hand.
• Pull back.

You are now in the Cradle position. Hold that position and turn the page.

THE MATTRESS

Notes

To make this formation, you start from the Cat's Cradle position.

TIPS:

When you take the string from your partner, keep your hands and fingers loose—the string needs to slide freely though your fingers.

Instructions

1. One partner holds the Cat's Cradle.

• The second partner reaches over and *from above* pinches the string between his thumbs and first fingers at the 2 points where the strings crisscross.

Very important: grab the string from the sides, not from the top and bottom.

2. Keeping fingers loose so the string can slide through them, the second partner pulls the strings *out* beyond the straight lines of the Cradle.

133

3. Still pinching the Xs, the second partner drops his hands under the Cradle and brings his thumbs and first fingers up through it.

• Thumbs and first fingers point skyward.

4. Second partner spreads his thumbs and first fingers outward as the first partner lowers his hands away from the string.

5. The second partner pulls the string taut. This position is called the "Mattress." Hold that position and turn the page.

PINKIES

Notes

• Start with the Mattress position.
• You'll make the same basic moves to get from the Mattress to Pinkies as you did going from the Cat's Cradle to the Mattress. But you end up with a completely different formation.

Instructions

1. One partner is holding the Mattress.
• The second partner reaches over and *from above* pinches the string between his thumbs and first fingers at the points where the strings crisscross.

• **Very important:** grab the string from the sides, not from the top and bottom.

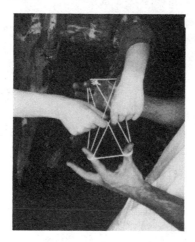

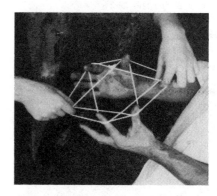

2. Keeping fingers loose so the string can slide through them, the second partner pulls the strings *out* beyond the straight lines of the Mattress.

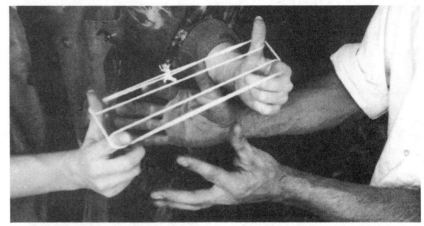

3. Still pinching the Xs, he drops his hands under the Mattress and brings his thumbs and first fingers up through it.

• Thumbs and first fingers point skyward.

4. Now the second partner spreads his thumbs and first fingers outward as the first partner lowers his hands away from the string.

5. The second partner pulls the string taut. This position is called "Pinkies."

Why is this called Pinkies? You'll find out in a second. Hold that position and turn the page.

THE UPTURNED CRADLE

Notes

In elementary school, this was considered one of the hardest moves in Cat's Cradle—probably because you need your pinkies in it, and kids' pinkies are small. Your pinkies still may not be limber, but now that your hands are bigger this should be pretty easy.

Instructions

1. One partner holds the Pinkies position. The second partner looks down at it. There are 2 strings in the middle.

2. The second partner reaches over and *from above* hooks the inside string opposite him with an upturned pinkie.

3. He pulls it toward himself until it crosses the other inside string.

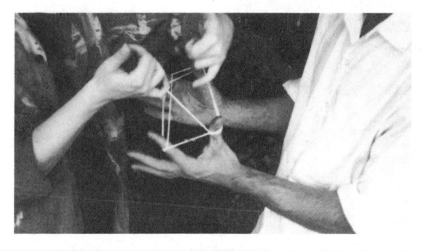

4. Then, with his other pinkie, he does the same in the other direction.

5. The inside strings are now crossed.

6. The second partner rotates his wrist and turns his hand over, facing downward through the holes created by the pinkies on each side.

7. He raises his thumbs and first fingers underneath the double strings on each side.
• Keep those pinkies hooked around the strings.

8. Second partner spreads his thumbs and first fingers outward as the first partner lowers his hands away from the string.

9. The second partner pulls the string taut. This position is the "Upturned Cradle." It looks like the Cat's Cradle turned upside down.

BACK TO THE MATTRESS

Notes

This move will bring you back to the Mattress position, beginning a perpetual cycle.

Instructions

1. One partner holds the Upturned Cradle.

• The second partner reaches over and *from below* pinches the string between his thumbs and first fingers at the points where the strings crisscross.

• **Very important:** grab the string from the sides, not from the top and bottom.

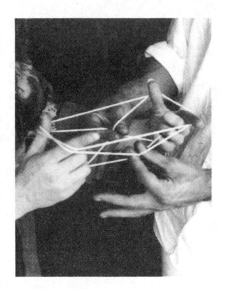

2. Keeping fingers loose so the string can slide through them, the second partner pulls the strings *out* beyond the straight lines of the Upturned Cradle.

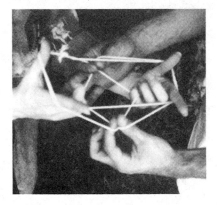

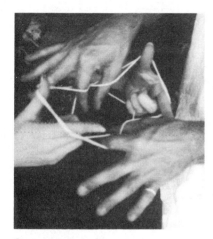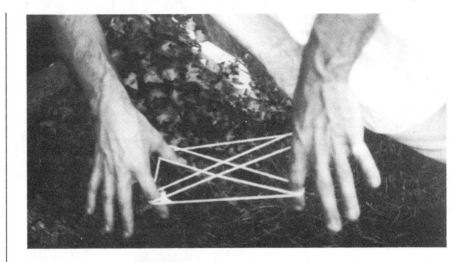

3. Still pinching the Xs, he pulls his hands up, over the Upturned Cradle, and brings his thumbs and first fingers down through it.
• Thumbs and first fingers point toward the floor.

4. Second partner spreads his thumbs and first fingers outward as the first partner lowers his hands away from the string.

5. The second partner pulls the string taut. Now you have the Mattress again. You can keep going as long as you want.

141

SOUNDS

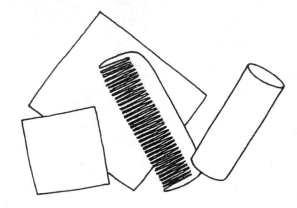

Background

Everybody likes to make noise. From the original human being's first grunts and groans to sophisticated classical music, we're constantly finding new ways to experiment with sound.

• Nothing in this section is particularly sophisticated...but it's all fun.

• These four soundmakers are strictly for kids—and for grown-ups who don't mind being a little silly.

You'll Need:

Your fingers (and a lot of patience)

A long blade of grass

Some tissue paper or wax paper

A cardboard tube from a roll of paper towels

A comb

2-FINGER WHISTLE

Notes

When you were a kid, there was always someone around who could stick his hands in his mouth and let out a superwhistle. It looked simple, but if you didn't know what you were doing, you just wound up with a mouthful of fingers. Very frustrating.

• Here are instructions. Even with them, it's still hard to get; but keep practicing, and it'll eventually make sense.

Instructions

1. Cover your teeth with your lips so you look like you have no teeth.

• Make sure your lips are tight around your teeth.

2. Move your tongue toward the back of your mouth, but don't touch the roof.

• Keep your tongue tight.

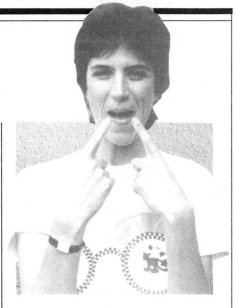

3. Put the first fingers of each hand into your mouth, almost to your first knuckle.

• Fingers are almost touching each other.

143

• Keep the fingers tight, too.

4. While biting down with your lips, gently bring your tongue forward and lightly touch your fingertips.

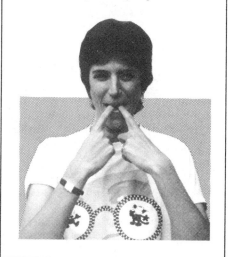

5. Blow. For some people, it takes lots of practice to get this. Others can get a whistling sound right away.
• If you have trouble with it, work on getting the opening correct. It's like a wind instrument, where everything should be vibrating against everything else. Keep adjusting till it feels right.

BLADE OF GRASS HONKER

Notes

Another childhood status symbol. Some lucky kids knew how to pick a blade of grass and make a loud noise with it. Now you can, too.

Instructions

1. Pick a wide blade of grass.
• Length depends on the length of your thumbs.

2. Hold your thumbs with their backs toward you.

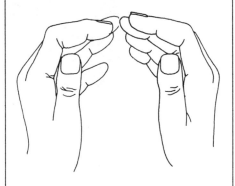

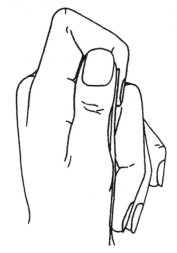

3. Lay the blade of grass against the outside edge of 1 thumb (inside as you look at it).

4. Keeping tension on the blade of grass, lay your other thumb against the first thumb. The blade of grass is tight between them.
• Notice the space between the 2 thumbs—that's the area you blow into.

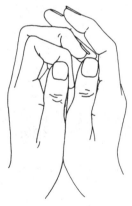

5. Blow gently. Your thumbs are now literally like a reed instrument—the noise is made by air vibrating the blade of grass.

• Experiment. The sounds you can make range from a goose in heat to the call of a woodpecker.

HOMEMADE KAZOOS

Notes

A kazoo is an instrument that turns humming into music. Normally, kazoos are made of metal, but you can make them out of household items. They're pretty amusing.

The Comb Kazoo

You need a pocket comb and a piece of wax paper or tissue paper.

Instructions

1. Fold the paper in half over the teeth of the comb.

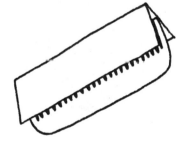

2. Fold your lips over your teeth and put the paper (and teeth of the comb) into your mouth.
•Don't get the paper wet.

3. As you move the comb back and forth in your mouth, hum. The paper vibrates and creates a kazoo.

147

Tube Kazoo

You need a cardboard tube (the inside of a roll of paper towels or toilet paper) and a piece of wax paper or tissue paper.

Instructions

1. Stretch the piece of wax or tissue paper over 1 end of the tube. Either hold it on or put a rubber band around it to keep it in place.

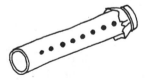

2. Put your mouth over (or in) the uncovered end of the tube and hum away.

• **Variation:** Using a nail, put about 8 holes in the tube, evenly spaced. Use them as finger holes to change the pitch of your humming.

COIN MAGIC

Background

• Coins have been around since the 8th century B.C. It's a safe bet that sleight-of-hand coin magic followed shortly after.

• Ancient Greeks and Romans had their own version of coin magic—they played a game in which they hid a coin under 1 of 3 cups, mixed the cups up, and challenged a person to guess which cup contained the coin.

• Beginning in the 1500s, the British and French wrote books about conveying money from 1 hand to another without being spotted. The principles described then are just as workable today; lots of magicians use them.

• This is a great way to entertain kids.

You'll Need:

A coin

• When you're learning to "palm" coins, you should start off with a quarter; larger coins are easier to hold on to and work with.

• With practice, you'll be able to use pennies and dimes.

• To practice your coin grips, you'll need small items you can pick up with the hand that is concealing the coin. Pencils, soda cans, and similarly sized objects will do.

Note: If you're wearing a ring, take it off. The click of the concealed coin against your ring is a dead giveaway that you're palming something.

BEGINNERS' TIPS

Notes

Before you can do any tricks with coins, you have to learn to conceal them. This section includes the 2 simplest ways of concealing, or "palming," a coin. It will take a little practice to make them work, but the good news is that you can practice anywhere, anytime—at a bus stop, while you're waiting in line at a supermarket, etc.

Technique

Always try to make the hand concealing the coin look as natural as possible. Resting your fingers on the table is a natural pose and won't raise any suspicion from your audience.

Distractions

An important part of "magic" is to distract your audience. You can do that effectively in 2 ways:
• With "patter," a running commentary while performing the trick.
• With motion. People's eyes follow motion, so you can direct their attention away from the hand with the coin by moving your other hand around and calling attention to it.

Of course, all of your efforts will be worthless if you show your audience the palm of your hand (and the coin in it). So always keep your palm turned away from onlookers.

THE CLASSIC PALM

Notes

This is the basic palming position.
• You will hold a coin in the center of your palm, using only your contracted hand muscles.
• It may seem tough-to-impossible at first. But with a little practice you'll be able to use different sizes of coins and look natural in the process.
• Don't squeeze or try too hard. All you need is the slightest amount of pressure to keep the coin in place. The coin isn't that heavy.

Instructions

1. Take a quarter and, using the first finger of 1 hand, place it firmly into

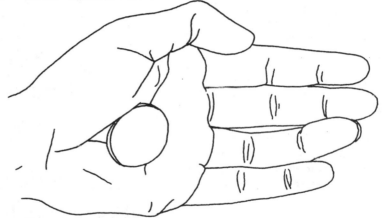

the palm of your other hand. Create a grip by contracting the thumb and pinky finger of the hand that's now holding the coin.

• The thumb mound serves as 1 "grip ledge," and the muscle group below your middle and third fingers grips from the other side.

2. To get used to having a coin in your palm, pick up other objects with that hand while your palm grips the coin.

• Try pulling up your sleeve, snapping your fingers, scratching your head, and making other movements to distract your audience.

3. When using this "palm" to perform a trick, use your coin-gripping hand to do a number of activities before you reveal the coin. This will throw your audience off.

4. Be sure to keep your palm toward your body so nobody can see the coin. With practice, you'll have them eating out of the palm of your hand.

THE FINGER PALM

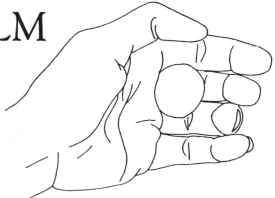

Notes

- This is the easiest "palm."
- You will conceal a coin in the fold between the knuckle and base of your middle and third fingers.
- Since our fingers naturally curl in toward our palms, you can create a natural cradle for a coin by resting your arms at your sides.

Instructions

1. Place the coin in the fold between the knuckle and base of your second and third fingers (see illustration).

- Try not to bend your fingers just curl them slightly, enough so they hold the coin in.

2. Practice your grip. Don't grip so hard that your hand looks unnatural. You should be able to snap your fingers and do other movements with that hand to distract your audience.

- When you first try this, you'll think your hand looks very unnatural as it palms the coin. However, when your hand hangs at your side (with the coin), it appears quite relaxed.

Note: With practice, you can move a coin from the Classic Palm to this position with a slight move of the hand.

THERE'S A COIN IN YOUR EAR

Notes

This is the trick everybody's uncle used to do: pulling a coin out of your ear, nose, or elbow.
• It takes a little flare, coordination, and practice. You should be comfortable with at least 1 of the "palm" positions before you start. This is 1 of those cases where your left hand has to know what your right is doing.

Instructions

1. Conceal a quarter using the Classic Palm or Finger Palm. The hand with the coin hangs by your side.

Use a few techniques to create the illusion that you're not holding anything in your hands (snapping fingers, general animated hand movement).
Note: This setup is important in order for the trick to work.

2. Point to your subject's nose, elbow, or ear with your free hand.
• Use some corny patter here—like "Have you got a quarter you can spare?" or "You know, I don't understand how you can hear with all that stuff in your ear," etc.

Harder (and Better) Alternative:
Reach into your pocket with your free hand and pull out a little change—3 or 4 coins is plenty. Let your audience see the coins. Say something like "Drat! Not enough. Say, can I borrow that quarter from you?"
• The extra coins are a big plus. They will add noise to the trick when you produce the quarter.

3. Now raise your coin-concealing hand to your subject's nose, elbow, or ear—whatever the "source" of the new coin happens to be.
• Don't forget the patter— e.g., "You don't mind if I borrow this quarter, do you?"

4. Cup your other hand below it. As you gently "milk" an earlobe, nose, or elbow for the coin, drop the coin into your cupped hand.
• Now you see the point of the loose change—if you've got a few coins in your cupped hand, the dropping coin will "clank" against them. It's an impressive effect.

THE GRAB & DROP

Notes

In this trick, you will hold the coin in 1 hand and pretend to grab it with the other hand.

• Actually, the coin will never leave the first hand—you'll be palming it.

• This is more complicated than the previous trick—it's going to take considerable practice—but it's impressive.

• This is "real" magic.

Instructions

1. Grasp the coin between your thumb and first 2 fingers.

How you hold the coin is the key to the trick....

• Your hand should be slightly curled, with all 4 fingers together (they provide a screen when you drop the coin into your palm).

• Your hand must be tilted slightly away from the audience. If you tilt it forward, the audience will be able to see into your palm and will see the coin in it.

• Hold the coin loosely, so it can drop easily, without forcing you to change hand position.

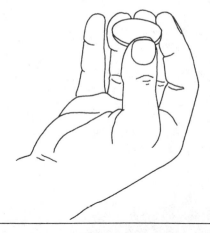

2. With a smooth motion, reach for the coin with your free hand, pretending to grasp it. Your thumb is underneath the coin, and the rest of your fingers curl over it but never touch it.

3. As the fingers of your free hand curl around the coin, it is temporarily out of sight. Use that moment to drop the coin into the palm of the hand that's already holding it.

• This is the motion that makes the trick. You have to be able to drop the coin directly into either the Classic Palm or the Finger Palm position to make the illusion work. (The Finger Palm is easier.)

• Practice palming the coin from a drop.

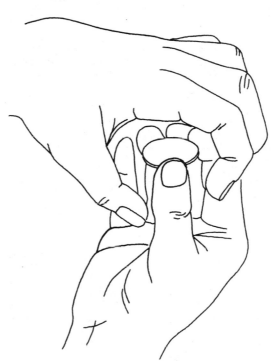

4. What about the other hand? You must close it so that it looks as though it's really holding the coin—and that takes practice.
• But you also have to use it to distract the audience. So, as you close it, immediately move it away from the hand that really holds the coin. Hold your empty hand in the air and say a

few "magic words" before it disappears, or pretend to toss it into thin air. Now the coin is "gone."

• Meanwhile, the hand with the coin hangs by your side. (Or you can surreptitiously put the coin in a pocket.)

5. Option: "Bring back" the coin the same way you did in the previous trick...or come up with a new method.

Acknowledgments

Thanks a million to:

• My editor, **Jodi Block**, for lots of reasons

• My other editor, **Shari Lesser-Wenk**, who magically appeared somewhere else

• **Michele Montez** and **Fritz Springmeyer** for their wonderful illustrations, encouragement, and miscellaneous support beyond the call of duty

• **Moira Hughes** for proofreading and formatting

• **Andrea** and **Dore** at Photolab

• **Doug and Doug at** Graphic Detail

• **Bonnie, Eleanor, Bill, Charlie, Gary**, and the rest of the insane models at Publisher's Group West

• **Pam** and the other models at EarthWorks

• **Effie** and **Walter**, my neighbor models

• **Jeff Abrahams** and friend, for help with some of the tricks.

• **Penelope** and **Mel**

• **Rachel Blau,** sneaky ghostwriter

• **Andrea Sohn**, designer and part-time model

• **The Dougans** (Mike and Andrea) and **Sharon**, the special spoonhangers

• **Ray Redel**, bubble man

• **Jay** and **Jamie** at Fifth Street Computer Services

• **Eve, June, Doug, Francis, Gail,** and the rest of the models at Determined Productions

• A bunch of people I just stopped on the street and shot (photos)

• **Hank Aaron**, my favorite baseball player when I was 7

• **Reddy Kilowatt**

• **Jack Mingo**

• **Professor Bubbles** and **Dr. Inflate-O**

• **Alphonse DeParnlo**, my invisible friend

COOL TRICK ALERT

As you might have guessed, I'm working on a book called (this is wildly creative, I know) *More Cool Tricks*.

And I need your help.

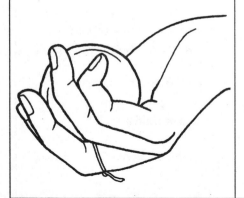

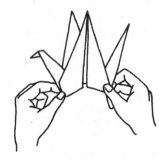

Everybody knows at least one really great trick that makes people smile. Why not share it? Send me a description of your favorite trick, and I'll give you credit in the book as a contributor—which is one of my cool tricks.

My address:
1400 Shatuck Ave., #25
Berkeley, CA 94709

Thanks!

160